GLOSSARY OF HOUSING TERMS

CMHC offers a wide range of housing information. Turn to the inside back cover for a listing of related publications.

Cette publication est aussi disponible en français sous le titre : *Glossaire des termes d'habitation* (LNH 1166).

Canadian Cataloguing in Publication Data

Main entry under title:

Glossary of housing terms

Rev. ed. of: A glossary of house-building and site-development terms, 1982.
Issued also in French under title: Glossaire des termes d'habitation.
ISBN 0-660-16699-2
Cat. no. NH15-159/1996E

1. Building — Dictionaries
2. House construction — Dictionaries.
I. Canada Mortgage and Housing Corporation.
II. Title: A glossary of house-building and site-development terms.

TH4812.G56 1996   690'.03   C96-980446-6

© 1982, Canada Mortgage and Housing Corporation
Revised 1997

Printed in Canada
Produced by CMHC

Preface

Formerly titled *A Glossary of House-Building and Site-Development Terms*, this invaluable reference text has been used for three decades by people in the housing industry and by university and college students enrolled in construction-related education programs.

Completely revised, this comprehensive, up-to-date glossary incorporates more than 300 new definitions to reflect current construction terminology. Selected illustrations from the companion volume, *Canadian Wood-Frame House Construction*, are included.

A

ABS *(ABS)* Acronym for acrylonitrile-butadiene-styrene. A type of rigid plastic used in plumbing pipes for drain, waste and vent systems. Can also be used for potable water.

AWG *(AWG)* The American Wire Gauge as applied to non-ferrous conductors and non-ferrous sheet metal.

above grade *(au-dessus du niveau du sol)* A term applied to any part of a structure or site feature that is above the adjacent finished ground level.

absorption field *(champ d'épuration, m., champ d'épandage, m.)* The area around a septic tank used for leaching liquid wastes.

abutment *(contrefort, m.)* A structure designed to receive a thrust; usually, the supporting structure at either end of an arch or bridge.

access hatch See hatch.

accessible design *(aménagement pour accès facile)* A house or amenity/product design that allows easier access for people with disabilities. For example, accessible sink. See barrier-free.

acid soil See soil.

acrylic latex sealant *(matériaux d'étanchéité acrylique, m.)* A paintable, water-based emulsion sealant used on non-porous surfaces such as aluminum, glass and ceramic tile and to seal joints in wood surfaces.

activated carbon air filter *(filtre à air à charbon actif, m.)* A filter activated by the absorption of moisture, when pollutant gases, attracted by the carbon, adhere to the filter.

adfreezing *(adhérence due au gel, f.)* The freezing of wet soil to below grade materials such as foundation walls or insulation, potentially causing those materials to move.

adjustable *(réglable, adj.)* An element of a house system, temporarily mounted on pilaster strips or brackets for manual movement, or attached to a handcrank or a small motor for mechanical movement. Adjustable systems may include cupboards, counters or vanities available in modules so they can suit current and future space requirements.

advanced combustion Wood burning technology that creates the conditions necessary to burn combustible gases without the use of catalysts.

aeration *(aération, f.)* **(1)** The adding of air. **(2)** In landscaping, the introduction of air into soil in order to improve it as a growing medium for plants.

aerator *(brise-jet, m.)* In plumbing, a fitting that controls the spray of water from a faucet.

aggregate *(agrégat, m.)* Material such as gravel, broken stone, or sand, with which cement and water are mixed to form concrete. See also mineral aggregate.

aggregate, coarse *(gros agrégat, m.)* An aggregate with particles of 5 mm in diameter and over; includes crushed stone and gravel.

aggregate, fine *(petit agrégat, m.)* An aggregate with particles smaller than 5 mm in diameter; includes sand.

air barrier *(pare-air, m.)* Material incorporated into the house envelope to retard the movement of air. Called air-vapour barrier when it retards air and moisture.

air chamber See plumbing terms.

air change *(renouvellement de l'air, m.)* The replacement of one complete house volume of air by either natural or mechanical means. Measured in air changes per hour (ac/h).

air conditioning See heating.

air-drying *(sec à l'air, adj.)* Seasoning under natural atmospheric conditions.

air duct *(conduit d'air, m.)* A pipe, tube, or passageway that conveys air; normally associated with heating, ventilating, and air conditioning.

air gap See plumbing terms.

air leakage *(fuite d'air, f.)* The uncontrolled flow of air through a building envelope or a component of a building envelope as a result of a pressure difference. See infiltration and exfiltration.

airlock entry *(entrée étanche à l'air, f.)* A vestibule sealed by a second interior door.

air permeability *(perméabilité à l'air, f.)* A measurement of the degree to which a building component allows air to pass through it when it is subjected to a differential pressure.

air pocket *(poche d'air, f.)* A space or void created by trapped air which accidentally occurs in concrete work or in a pipe line.

air pressure *(pression d'air, f.)* The force per unit of area exerted by the atmosphere. It can have two components: static pressure, which is caused by the weight of a column of atmosphere, and dynamic pressure, caused by air flow.

air requirements See heating terms.

air sealing *(étanchéisation à l'air, f.)* The application of weather stripping such as caulking and expanding foam to close off small cracks and spaces at windows and doors and on walls and ceilings to reduce air leakage and consequent heat loss.

air shutters See heating terms.

air space *(vide d'air, m.)* A cavity or space in walls, windows, or other enclosed parts of a building between various structural members.

air-supported structure *(structure gonflable, f.)* A structure consisting of a pliable membrane which achieves and maintains its shape by internal air pressure.

airtightness *(étanchéité à l'air, f.)* The ability of the house envelope to resist infiltration and exfiltration of air.

air-to-air heat exchanger *(échangeur de chaleur air-air, m.)* Older version of a Heat Recovery Ventilator (HRV). Its purpose is to warm incoming fresh air using the heat of stale air being expelled. See HRV.

air-vapour barrier See air barrier.

airway *(passage d'air, m.)* The space left between roof insulation and roof decking to allow free movement of air.

air well *(puits d'air, m.)* A space within a building, enclosed by walls, partially or totally open to the outside air at the roof, and designed to ventilate service rooms such as bathrooms and kitchens.

alarm system *(système de sécurité, m.)* A set of devices that triggers an alert in the case of intrusion, smoke, fire or the presence of a specific chemical in the air.

alternating current See electrical terms.

alpha track detector *(détecteur alpha, m.)* A device that detects radon when radioactive emissions of alpha particles produced by the gas damage a plastic sheet.

ambient temperature *(température ambiante, f.)* the temperature of air outside a building or within a room.

amendment *(amendement, m.)* In landscaping, a substance added to a soil to improve its physical properties, such as texture.

amenity area *(aire d'agrement, f.)* An area within the boundaries of a multi-unit project intended for recreational purposes which may include landscaped site areas, patios, common areas, communal lounges or swimming pools.

ampere See electrical terms.

ampacity See electrical terms.

anchor bolt *(boulon d'ancrage, m.)* A steel bolt used to secure a structural member against uplift. It is usually deformed at one end to ensure a good grip in the concrete or masonry in which it is embedded.

anchor slots *(rainure d'ancrage, f.)* Perforation through which a bolt can be inserted to secure a building structure to one of various wall components, such as bottom track, bottom plate or shelf angle (for brick veneer).

angle bead *(baguette d'angle, f.)* A small moulding placed at an external angle formed by plastered surfaces in order to preserve the corner from accidental fracture.

angle iron *(cornière, f.)* An L-shaped steel section frequently used to support masonry over a window or door opening.

anhydrous lime *(chaux anhydre, f.)* Quicklime.

annual *(plante annuelle, f.)* A plant with a life span of one year's duration.

annual growth ring *(anneau de croissance annuelle, m.)* The ring seen on the transverse section of a piece of wood indicating yearly growth. Also referred to as a grain. See also year ring.

apartment *(appartement, m.)* A room or suite of rooms used as living quarters. A dwelling unit of a multi-family house. See dwelling, multiple.

apartment building *(immeuble d'appartements, m.)* A type of multiple dwelling comprising three or more dwelling units with shared entrances and other essential facilities and services and with shared exit facilities above the first storey.

appliance *(appareil, m.)* **(1)** A piece of household equipment run by gas or electricity; **(2)** In plumbing, a receptacle or piece of equipment that receives or collects water, liquids or sewage and discharges it into an indirect waste pipe or fixture.

apron *(allège, f., tablier, m.)* **(1)** A plain or moulded finish piece below the stool of a window, installed to cover the rough edge of the wall finish. **(2)** The extension of the concrete floor of a garage or other structure beyond the face of the building.

aquifier *(couche aquifère, f.)* An underground formation of sands, gravel, or fractured or porous rock, which is saturated with water, and which supplies water for wells and springs.

aquastat See heating terms.

arcade *(arcade, f.)* A row of arches supported by columns, which may be either attached to a building or free-standing.

arch *(arche, f.)* A form of structure with a curved shape spanning an opening. It is supported by piers, abutments, or walls and is used to support weight and resist pressure.

arch brick *(brique-claveau, f.)* A brick having a wedge shape; also one with a curved face suitable for wells and other circular work.

architrave *(chambranle, m.)* Mouldings around openings and certain other locations to conceal joints or for decorative purposes.

area *(aire, f.)* The surface within specific boundaries.

    building *(aire du bâtiment, f.)* The maximum projected horizontal area of the building at or above grade within the outside perimeter of the exterior walls or within the outside perimeter of exterior walls and the centre line of fire walls.

    floor *(aire de plancher, f.)* The space on any storey of a building between exterior walls and required firewalls, including the space occupied by interior walls and partitions, but not including exits and vertical service spaces that pierce the storey.

    net room *(aire nette d'une pièce, f.)* The floor area of a room measured from finished wall to finished wall.

area drain See plumbing terms.

areaway *(puits de lumière, m.)* An open sub-surface space, adjacent to a building, used to admit light or air, or as a means of access to an area or floor level below grade.

armoured cable See electrical terms, cable, armoured.

artificial stone *(similipierre, f.)* A special concrete unit, sometimes artificially coloured, intended to resemble natural stone, made by mixing chippings and dust of natural stone with Portland cement and water. This mixture is placed in moulds and cured before use.

asbestos *(amiante, f.)* A variety of fibrous silicate materials, mainly calcium magnesium silicate. Used as a heat insulator or for fire-resistance purposes. A carcinogen.

asbestos cement *(amiante-ciment, m.)* A fire-resisting weatherproof building material made from Portland cement and asbestos. It is manufactured in various forms such as plain sheets, corrugated sheets, shingles and pipes.

ash *(cendre, f.)* The solid waste remaining after combustion of a solid fuel.

ashlar See stonework, kinds of.

asphalt (bituminous) *(asphalte, m.)* A dark substance which is insoluble in water and used extensively in building for waterproofing, roof coverings, in the manufacture of shingles and floor tiles, and in paints. See also paving.

astragal *(astragale, f.)* A small plain or ornamental moulding.

at grade *(au niveau du sol, adj.)* A term applied to the part of a structure or site feature which is located at the same elevation as the adjacent ground level.

atmospheric burner *(brûleur atmosphérique, m.)* A gas burner with no fan or blower, that relies solely on natural draft to inspirate combustion air.

atrium *(atrium, m.)* An enclosed interior court, one or more levels high, onto which other rooms may open.

attic *(attique, m., vide sous comble, m.)* The space between the upper floor ceiling and roof or between a dwarf partition and a sloping roof. Also called roof space.

attic hatch *(trappe d'attique, f.)* The opening to an attic.

automatic *(automatique, adj.)* A housing element, such as a door or window, that uses hydraulic or electrical systems to facilitate opening and closing.

awning *(auvent, m.)* A rooflike cover for a window or a porch. See also window types and sash types.

azimuth *(azimut, m.)* The bearing or direction of a horizontal line measured clockwise from true North and expressed in degrees.

B

BRI See building-related illness.

BTU See British thermal unit.

B-vent See chimney types.

Bacharach smoke number See heating terms.

bachelor apartment See bachelor dwelling.

bachelor dwelling *(garçonnière, f., studio, m.)* A unit, with not more than one bedroom, providing living, sleeping, eating, food preparation, and sanitary facilities.

back bedding See back putty.

backdrafting (flow reversal) *(refoulement, m., siphonnage, m.)* The reverse flow of outdoor air into a building through the barometric damper, draft hood or burner unit as a result of chimney blockage or a pressure differential greater than can be drawn by the chimney. Backdrafting causes smell, smoke or toxic gases to escape into the interior of a building. "Cold" backdrafting occurs when the chimney is acting as an air inlet but there is no burner operation. "Hot" backdrafting occurs when the hot flue gas products are prevented from exhausting by flue reversal.

backfill *(remblai, m.)* Material used after excavation for filling in a trench or the gap around a foundation wall.

backflow See plumbing terms.

backflow preventer See plumbing terms.

backing *(fond de clouage, m.)* Material used to provide reinforcement or a nailing surface for certain finish materials.

back pressure See plumbing terms.

back pressure backflow See plumbing terms.

back putty *(mastic de fond, m.)* Mastic material placed in rabbets before installing glass to provide a bed for the glass.

back siphonage See plumbing terms.

back up *(mur de support, m.)* In veneer wall systems, a non-loadbearing steel-stud or concrete-masonry wall placed inside the exterior veneer of a high-rise building to resist lateral loads and to support insulation, air and vapour barriers, and interior finish.

back vent See plumbing terms.

back-water valve See plumbing terms.

baffle *(chicane, f.)* An object placed in an appliance to change the direction of, or retard the flow of air, gas-air mixtures or flue gases.

balance See window, parts of.

balcony *(balcon, m.)* A gallery or platform, either cantilevered or supported, that projects from the wall of a building and is enclosed by a balustrade or railing.

balled and burlapped *(emmotté, entoilé, adj.)* Plant material whose roots have been protected during digging with a solid ball of earth and which is wrapped in burlap for shipment.

balloon framing See wood framing.

baluster *(balustre, m.)* Vertical members in a balustrade between the handrail and the treads or stringers in a staircase.

balustrade *(balustrade, f.)* A protective barrier approximately 900 - 1200 mm high at the edge of openings in floors or at the side of stairs, landings, balconies, mezzanines, galleries, raised walk ways, or other locations to prevent accidental falls from one level to another. Such a barrier may be solid or may have openings through it.

banister *(main courante, f.)* The handrail of a staircase.

bare roots *(à racines nues)* Plants with roots left unprotected by such means as burlap.

barge board *(bordure de pignon, f.)* The finished board covering the gable rafter on a gable roof. See also facer board, verge board.

barometric damper or barometric draft regulator *(régulateur de tirage, m.)* A device which functions to maintain a desired draft in the appliance by automatically reducing excess chimney draft to the desired value.

barrier-free *(accès facile (pour), m.)* Housing designs that minimize or eliminate restrictions to occupant movement, usually included in homes for seniors or people with disabilities. Example: wider hallways, wider doorways, ramps.

baseboard *(plinthe, f.)* Interior trim at the intersection of the wall and the floor.

baseboard heater *(radiateur-plinthe, m.)* See heating.

base course *(assise de base, f.)* In masonry, the first or bottom course of masonry units.

base line *(ligne de départ, f.)* A line of known length and position which is used as a basis for establishing the locations of buildings, paths, and other site installations.

basement *(sous-sol, m.)* The lower storey of a building below or partly below ground level.

Base moulding: (A) two-piece; (B) one-piece.

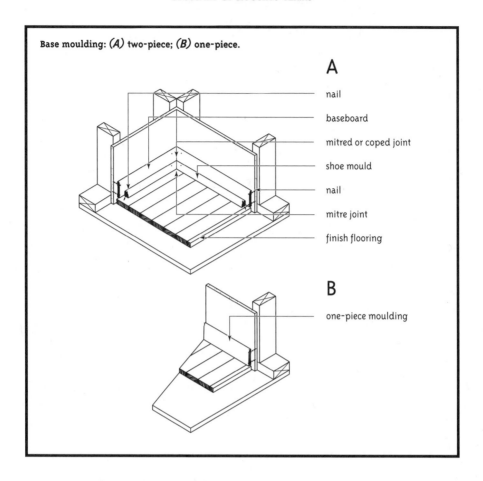

A

nail

baseboard

mitred or coped joint

shoe mould

nail

mitre joint

finish flooring

B

one-piece moulding

base moulding *(moulure de socle, f.)* Any moulding placed at the base of a column, wall, etc. See also shoe mould.

bat *(tuileau, m.)* In masonry, a piece of brick with one end whole, the other end broken off.

bathroom *(salle de bains, f.)* A room used for personal care, usually containing a sink and a toilet, often with bathtub and/or shower.

bathtub *(baignoire, f.)* A fixed, open-topped tank used for bathing.

bathtub, roman *(baignoire romaine, f.)* A deep, sunken bathtub, generally placed away from a wall or free standing.

bathtub, whirlpool *(bain tourbillon, bain hydromasseur, m.)* A deep bathtub equipped with a pump that recirculates water.

batt *(natte, f.)* A semi-rigid section of mineral wool or glass-fibre anchored to paper which is fixed between framed members. See also friction-fit batt.

batten *(tasseau, m.)* A narrow strip of wood used to cover joints between boards or panels.

batter *(reculement, m.)* A receding upward slope; normally applied to a wall or structural member where the thickness diminishes towards the top.

batter board *(planche de repère, f.)* Board set adjacent to an excavation and used to level and align the work.

bay *(baie, f.)* One of the intervals or spaces into which a building is divided by columns, piers, or division walls.

bay window See window types.

beam *(poutre, f.)* A horizontal structural member supported at two or more points, but not throughout its full length.

beam pocket *(retrait à poutre, f.)* A notch or space normally in a masonry or concrete wall in which the end of the beam is supported.

bearing capacity *(capacité portante, f.)* The applied load per unit area of surface of any structure or soil, which the structure or soil can support.

bearing plate *(plaque d'appui, f.)* A plate provided to distribute the load imposed by a specific member or members. Normally a steel plate set on concrete or masonry to support a structural member.

bearing wall See partition.

bed *(lit, m.)* (1) Generally any horizontal surface which has been prepared to receive the element(s) it will support. (2) In masonry, the horizontal layer of mortar on which each course of masonry is laid.

bed joints *(joints d'assise, m.)* (1) The horizontal joints in brick-work or masonry. (2) The radiating joints in an arch.

bed-moulding *(moulure de corniche, f.)* Any moulding used to cover the joint at the intersection of a wall and projecting cornice.

bedrock *(roche mère, f.)* Solid rock underlying surficial material; may be exposed at the surface.

bedroom *(chambre à coucher, f.)* A room used primarily for sleeping.

below grade *(au-dessous du niveau du sol)* A term applied to any part of a structure or site feature that is below the adjacent finished ground level.

belvedere See outdoor spaces.

benchmark *(borne-repère, f.)* A surveyor's mark cut in a durable post, block, or other device to indicate a definite point from which elevations are set.

bending stress *(contrainte en flexion, f.)* A force causing a deflection in shape or position of any member of a structure.

bent See truss terminology.

berm *(talus, m.)* An earth embankment in the form of a linear mound; often combined with fencing or planting to create a visual or sound barrier.

bevel *(biseau, m.)* The sloping surface formed when two surfaces meet at an angle other than a right angle.

bevel siding *(bardage à clin, m.)* Boards normally 100-300 mm in width tapering to a thin edge, and used as covering for sides of buildings, the thicker edge overlapping the thinner edge.

bib *(robinet d'arrosage, m.)* A tap or faucet which has been threaded for connection of a hose. Also known as a hose bib.

bidet *(bidet, m.)* A shallow basin similar to a toilet, equipped with a faucet and used for washing the genital area.

biennial *(plante biennale, f.)* A plant with a life span of two seasons.

bitumen *(bitume, m.)* The term covering numerous mixtures of hydrocarbons such as those found in asphalt and mineral pitch.

bleeding *(exsudation, f.)* An exudation of resin, gum, creosote, or other substance from lumber.

bleed water *(eau de ressuage, f.)* Excess water in a concrete mixture which surfaces after placing.

blemish *(tache, f.)* Anything marring the appearance of wood.

blind-nailing *(clouage dissimulé, m.)* Nailing in such a way that the nailheads are not finally visible on the face of the work.

blistering See paint.

block *(bloc, m.)* In masonry, a manufactured concrete unit in which various types of aggregate may be used. See also construction types.

block, cellular *(bloc cellulaire, m.)* A block having uniformly distributed pores throughout its mass.

block plan *(plan en bloc, m.)* A plan of a building site showing the outlines of existing and proposed buildings.

blocked vent shut-off system *(système de soupapes d'arrêt pour évents obstrués)* A system designed to interrupt appliance main burner gas flow if the appliance venting system is totally blocked.

blower door *(soufflerie de porte, f.)* A large fan, which when installed in an exterior doorway, can be used to depressurize a building or house to measure airtightness. Blower doors can also be used as tools to identify areas of air infiltration to guide and direct air sealing measures during a weatherization.

blower door test *(essai à la soufflerie de porte, m.)* A diagnostic test using a blower door to measure the airtightness of a building. Results are usually given in air changes per hour (acph or ac/h). Blower door tests are useful in assessing building envelopes, sizing ventilation and determining indoor air quality.

blowing *(piqûre, f.)* A plastering defect that results when a conical piece is blown out of a finished surface because moisture in the plaster has mixed with an imperfectly slaked mixture of quicklime. Also called pitting.

blue-stain *(bleuissement, m.)* A bluish discolouration of lumber, caused by certain fungi, which seldom penetrates beyond the sapwood.

board See lumber.

board foot *(pied-planche, m.)* An Imperial measure unit defined as the volume of a piece of wood one inch thick, one foot wide, and one foot long, equivalent to 144 cubic inches (2,360 cubic centimeters).

bollard *(butoir, m.)* A wooden, concrete, or metal post used to prevent vehicles from entering a pedestrian area.

bond *(appareil, m.)* In masonry, the pattern in which bricks or blocks are laid to tie the individual units together so that the entire wall they comprise will tend to act as a complete unit.

borrow pit *(emprunt de terre, m.)* An excavation from which earth materials are obtained for use as fill.

botanical name *(nom botanique, m.)* The scientific name of a plant, expressed in Latin. Includes genus, species, and variety.

bottom plate *(lisse basse, f.)* The lower horizontal member of a wood frame wall nailed to the bottom of the wall studs and to the floor framing members.

bottom track *(rail inférieur, m.)* In steel stud wall assembly, the bottom structure which holds the studs and is attached to the floor.

boulevard strip *(accotement, m.)* The portion of a street right-of-way that lies between the curb and the property line; also applied to a grassed or planted area between curb and sidewalk. See also median strip.

bow window See window terminology.

bowing *(cambrure, f.)* A deviation from a straight line, measured at the point ot greatest distance from the straight line. Often applied to lumber.

box beam *(poutre à caisson, f.)* A beam made of plywood on a lumber framework.

box column *(poteau à caisson, m.)* A built-up hollow column of square or rectangular section generally used in porch construction.

box connector See connector, box.

box gutter *(gouttière de bois, f.)* A wooden gutter usually lined with metal having upright sides, sometimes called concealed gutter.

boxed track *(rail caissonné, m.)* A method of assembling steel stud walls in which studs are secured to an inverted top (inner) track held by an outer track attached to the ceiling, so that the backup wall is free of vertical loads while it supports horizontal loads.

brace *(écharpe, f.)* In carpentry, an inclined piece of timber used in walls and in trussed partitions or in framed roofs to form a triangle and thereby stiffen the framing. When a brace supports a rafter, it is called a strut.

braced framing *(ossature contreventée, f.)* Supported framework of a house, especially at corners.

bracing *(contreventement, m.)* Ties used for supporting and strengthening various types of buildings.

brads See nail, types.

branch (plumbing) See plumbing terms.

branch circuit See electrical terms.

branch vent See plumbing terms.

breaking joints *(rompre les joints, v.)* (1) The manner of laying masonry units so as to prevent vertical joints in adjacent courses from lining up. (2) The distribution of joints in boards, flooring, lath and panels so no two adjacent end-joints are directly in line.

breech or breaching *(culotte, f.)* A flue pipe or chamber for receiving flue gases from one or more flue connections and for discharging these gases through a single flue connection.

breech pipe *(tuyau de culotte, m.)* A short pipe with one end permanently mortared into the breech of a masonry chimney, and the other end for the attachment of a flue pipe. The flue gases come into contact with the breech pipe.

breezeway *(passage extérieur recouvert, m.)* A covered passageway between a house and an auxiliary building.

brick *(brique, f.)* A masonry unit usually made from fired clay.

brick construction See construction types.

brick facing See construction types: brick veneer.

brick ties *(agrafe à brique, f.)* Metal straps that provide lateral support to the brick veneer of a building by transmitting lateral loads to the backup wall.

brick veneer See construction types.

bridging See wood framing.

bridging, cross See cross-bridging.

British thermal unit *(unité thermale britannique, f.)* Or BTU. The amount of heat required to raise the temperature of one pound of pure water one degree Fahrenheit. One BTU is the equivalent of 1,055.06 joules (Nm).

broken joints See joints.

broom finish *(fini au balai, m.)* A method of finishing concrete surfaces in which a stiff broom is used to rub the still-wet surface, giving it a rough texture and linear pattern.

building area See area.

building drain See plumbing terms.

building envelope See envelope.

building orientation *(orientation du bâtiment, f.)* The siting of a building on a lot. The term is generally used when discussing solar orientation, which is the siting of a building with respect to access to solar radiation.

building paper *(papier de construction, m.)* A sheathing paper usually applied underneath or behind exterior finish materials in wood-frame construction to act as a moisture barrier and air barrier. The material should be able to breathe, so as not to act as a vapour barrier.

building related illness Acronym, BRI. *(MCM Maladie causée par le milieu)* A medical condition caused by a building environment and frequently involving an infection; differs from Sick Building Syndrome in that a building related illness is substantiated by clinical and laboratory findings. For example, Legionnaire's Disease, in which micro-organisms are spread by air conditioning systems.

building sewer See plumbing terms.

building site *(emplacement de construction, m.)* A parcel of land suitable for building, or on which a building is being built or may be built. Also called plot.

building storm drain See plumbing terms.

building storm sewer See plumbing terms.

building trap See plumbing terms.

built-in transfer equipment *(matériel de déplacement encastré, m.)* A system designed to aid people with mobility disabilities, consisting of ceiling-mounted tracks, lifting devices, a control panel and switches, an electric motor, a power supply and a back-up battery.

built-up roof *(couverture multicouche, f.)* A roof covering consisting of layers of roofing felt laid in pitch or asphalt. The top is finished with crushed stone, gravel, or a cap sheet. Generally used on flat or low-pitched roofs.

bulkhead *(construction hors-toit, f., trappe inclinée, f.)* **(1)** A structure above the roof of any part of a building enclosing a stairway, tank, elevator machinery, or ventilating apparatus, or any part of a shaft that extends above the roof; **(2)** a sloping door or doors affording entrance to a cellar from outside a building.

bull float *(aplanissoir, m.)* A board of wood, aluminum or magnesium, mounted on a pole which is used to spread and smooth freshly placed horizontal concrete surfaces.

bull-nose *(rive arrondie, f.)* A rounded corner used to obtain a decorative and finished appearance.

burl *(loupe, f.)* A distortion of wood grain, usually caused by abnormal growth due to injury to the tree.

burner, atmospheric See atmospheric burner.

burner unit *(brûleur, m.)* That part of an appliance or furnace that produces fire or heat.

butt *(contrefort, m., renfort, m.)* A structural element built perpendicular to a wall in order to resist lateral thrusts.

butt joint See joints.

butterfly damper *(registre à papillon, m.)* A plate or blade installed in a duct, breeching or flue connection which rotates on an axis.

butyl rubber sealant *(joint en caoutchouc butyl, m.)* A paintable, synthetic rubber sealant that bonds to most surfaces, particularly to metal and masonry.

C

CEBus (Consumer Electronic Bus) *(pas d'équivalent en français)* A home automation protocol developed by the Electronics Industry Association as a public communications standard. CEBus uses two-way communications transmitted via any available transmission media (twisted pair wiring, coaxial cable, infra red, fibre optics, etc.). See home automation.

CFC (Chlorofluorocarbons) *(CFC)* Chemicals used in refrigerants, solvents and blowing agents for many rigid insulations. When released in the air, they are linked to ozone depletion in the atmosphere.

cable See electrical terms.

cable, armoured See electrical terms.

caliper *(calibre, m.)* **(1)** An instrument with two adjustable legs used for measuring the thickness of objects. **(2)** The diameter of the trunk of a tree, normally measured at a height of 300 mm above grade.

camber *(cambrure, f.)* The amount of upward curve given to an arch, arch bar, beam, or girder to prevent the member from becoming concave due to its own weight or the weight of the load it must carry.

camber arch *(arc cambré, m.)* An arch, a flat horizontal extrados and a cambered intrados with a rise of about one per cent.

cambium *(cambium, m.)* The layer of tissue just beneath the bark of a tree, in which the new wood and bark cells of each year's growth develop.

canopy *(auvent, m.)* A roof-like structure over an opening in an exterior wall.

cantilever *(porte-à-faux, m.)* Astructural member unsupported at one end which projects outward to carry the weight of a structure above, such as a balcony.

cant strip *(chanlatte, f.)* A wedge or triangular-shaped piece generally installed on flat roofs around the perimeter or at the junction of the roof and adjoining wall.

cap *(couronnement, m.)* A block or other covering, plain or moulded, forming the top of a wall, pier, newel post, or column; a wall coping, chimney cap. See also wood framing.

capillary action *(action capillaire, f.)* The process of water movement through materials with tiny pores.

capillary flow. Or capillarity *(capillarité, f.)* The flow of liquid within small pore passages in a material. Also called wicking. The water transport mechanism is what allows a sponge to soak up water.

capital *(chapiteau, m.)* The upper part of a column, pilaster, pier, etc. widened for decorative purposes or to distribute loads.

carbon dioxide *(dioxyde de carbone, m.)* An odorless, invisible gas occuring naturally in small concentrations in the atmosphere. Produced by animals as part of the respiratory process in nature, it can also be emitted by machines, especially combustion machines. Dangerous if present in high concentrations.

carbon filter *(filtre à charbon, m.)* A device employing a carbon block or carbon granules to remove some particulates from water. Activated carbon in a carbon filter removes unwanted, volatile chemicals such as chlorine, toxic gases, solvents, pesticides and some trace minerals. Available in one or two part filter units, they do not remove sediments.

carbon monoxide (CO) *(monoxyde de carbone, m.)* A colourless, odourless, and toxic gas produced during the combustion process that can be produced by kerosene heaters, wood burning appliances, unvented gas appliances and automobiles.

carbon monoxide detector *(détecteur de monoxyde de carbone, m.)* A device used to detect the presence of carbon monoxide.

carpet *(moquette, f., tapis, m.)* A fabric floor covering.

carpet terminology *(moquette, f. (terminologie))*

> **cut pile** *(velours coupé, m.)* Pile composed of cut yarn attached to primary fabric backing and protected by secondary latex-coated fabric backing.

> **glue-down** *(pose flottante, f.)* A type of carpet with a cushion layer of foam backing and secured directly to the subfloor with latex adhesive.

> **loop pile** *(poils bouclés, m.)* Pile composed of looped yarn woven through primary fabric backing and protected by secondary latex-coated fabric backing.

> **stretch-in** *(moquette étirée, f.)* A type of carpet with a separate undercushion stapled to the subfloor, then stretched and hooked onto strips nailed to the edges of the subfloor.

carport *(abri d'auto, m.)* A shelter for a car, adjacent to a dwelling, roofed but not completely enclosed.

carriage bolt *(boulon de carrosserie, m.)* A round-headed bolt used in the assembly of wooden members when the bolt head will be exposed to view.

casement See window types.

casing *(encadrement, m.)* A form of trim used around window and door openings.

catalyst *(catalyseur, m.)* A substance that effects a reaction without being consumed in the process. For example, the catalyst in a catalytic combustion appliance is a coated ceramic honeycomb through which the exhaust gas is routed.

catch basin *(bassin collecteur, m.)* A chamber in a drainage system designed to intercept solids and prevent their entrance into the system.

cathedral ceiling See ceiling.

caulk *(calfeutrer, v.)* To make tight with a sealing material.

caulking *(calfeutrage, m., matériau d'étanchéité, m.)* Material with widely different chemical compositions used to make a seam or joint air-tight or watertight. All caulking uses solvents that can give off fumes, necessitating adequate ventilation during application.

cavity wall *(mur creux, m.)* A masonry or concrete wall constructed of two separate thicknesses with a minimum 50 mm cavity between and tied together by metal ties or bonding units.

ceiling *(plafond, m.)* The overhead inside surface of a room.

> **cathedral ceiling** *(plafond cathédrale, m.)* Ceilings that follow the roof slope where there is no attic included. May be framed with conventional lumber or pre-manufactured trusses.

> **coffered ceiling** *(plafond à caissons, m.)* A ceiling featuring recesses in a regular pattern.

> **coved ceiling** *(plafond à gorge, m.)* A ceiling which is formed at the edges to give a hollow curve from wall to ceiling instead of a sharp angle of intersection.

> **vaulted ceiling** *(plafond à voutes, m.)* A ceiling employing high arches.

ceiling beam See truss terminology.

ceiling joist See joists.

ceiling outlet See electrical terms.

cellar *(cave, f.)* That portion of a building between two floor levels which is partly or wholly underground and which has more than one-half of its height, from finished floor to finished ceiling, below grade.

cellulose fibre insulation *(isolant cellulosique, m.)* Insulation made from shredded newsprint treated with chemicals that resists fire and fungal growth and inhibits corrosion.

cement *(ciment, m.)* A grey, powdered substance produced from a burned mixture chiefly of clay and limestone; used in making concrete or mortar.

cement grout *(coulis de ciment, m.)* A mortar of cement mixed with water and sand to the consistency of thick cream; used for bedding bearing plates, setting anchor bolts, and filling and smoothing foundation cracks.

cement mortar *(mortier de ciment, m.)* A mortar in which the cement material is primarily Portland cement.

central heating See heating.

centre line *(axe, m., ligne de centre, f.)* A line, actual or assumed, which divides symmetrically a surface or object; used as a reference for measurement.

centre to centre *(entraxes, m.)* In taking measurements, a term meaning on centre (ie. the middle of the width) as in the spacing of joists, studding, or other structural parts.

ceramic fibre liner See heating terms.

ceramic tiles See tile.

cesspool See plumbing terms.

chain-link fence *(clôture à mailles de chaîne, f.)* A woven fence, normally made of steel wire, attached to posts and rails.

chalking *(farinage, m.)* A condition in which paint deteriorates by oxidation to form a chalk-like powder. Chalking may contaminate surrounding soil.

chamfer *(chanfrein, m.)* A sloping or bevelled edge.

channel iron *(profilé, m.)* A steel section having a web with two flanges extending in the same direction.

charcoal detector *(détecteur au charbon, m.)* A device to detect radon gas. The most common is a container that allows radon gas to enter and be absorbed by the charcoal.

check *(fente, f.)* A longitudinal crack in timber that may be caused by too rapid seasoning.

checking See paint.

check rails *(traverses de rencontre, f.)* The meeting rails in sliding or double-hung window sashes which meet when closed and are of sufficient thickness to overlap.

check valve See plumbing terms.

chimney *(cheminée, f.)* A structure of brick, stone, concrete, metal, or other noncombustible material, providing a housing for one or more flues which carry products of combustion to the outdoors.

chimney types *(cheminées, f. (types))*

    air-cooled *(refroidie par air)* A chimney which uses a flow of air between inner and outer layers to keep the outer surface cool. Air-cooled chimneys are approved for use in some factory-built fireplaces that are used for decorative purposes. Air-cooled chimneys are not suitable for cold climates or well sealed houses. Wood-burning appliances should never be connected to air-cooled chimneys.

    B-vent *(évent de type B, m.)* A prefabricated double-walled metal chimney with aluminum inner liner, designed solely for use with gaseous fuels.

    bracket masonry *(supports de maçonnerie, m.)* Brick chimneys built on wooden supports within a wall of a house; common in older houses. Bracket masonry chimneys cannot be upgraded to meet current building code requirements. Also called bracket chimney.

    factory-built *(préfabriquée, adj.)* A chimney consisting entirely of factory-made parts, each designed to be assembled with the other without requiring fabrication on the building site.

chimney types (continued)

masonry *(maçonnerie, f.)* Chimneys that consist of a clay tile liner surrounded by brick or stone. Those built to building code regulations may be used with wood burning appliances.

metal *(métallique)* Factory-built metal chimneys common in new homes; can be used with gas, oil and wood-burning appliances. A 650 degree Celsius metal chimney, designed to withstand high temperatures, is a requirement for solid fuel or wood-burning appliances.

type-A *(type A, m.)* A double-walled, factory-built metal chimney used for oil and gas furnaces. It is no longer considered suitable for wood-burning appliances.

unlined masonry *(maçonnerie non chemisée, f.)* Older masonry chimneys not lined with clay tiles, firebrick or stainless steel; not suitable for wood-burning appliances.

chimney cap *(lanterne, f.)* A protective covering or housing for the top of a chimney intended for preventing the entry of rain, snow, animals, birds, etc. and for preventing wind induced downdrafts.

chimney connector See chimney flue pipe.

chimney draft *(tirage de la chemisée, m.)* The available natural draft of the chimney, measured at or near the base of the chimney.

chimney thimble *(fourreau de cheminée, m.)* The connector that joins the vent connector through the wall to the chimney and liner.

chimney flashing *(solin de cheminée, m.)* Any kind of metal or composition material placed around a chimney where it penetrates through a roof, to cover the joint and prevent water from entering.

chimney flue pipe *(conduit de cheminée, m.)* A passage housed in a chimney through which products of combustion are carried from a fuel burning appliance to the exterior. Also called chimney lining.

chimney lining See chimney flue pipe.

chimney saddle *(solin en dos d'âne, m.)* A peaked flashing between a chimney and the roof to shed moisture around the chimney. See also cricket.

chord *(membrure, f.)* The principal member of a truss, either top or bottom.

chord members See truss terminology.

chronotherm *(thermostat intelligent, m.)* A type of thermostat that takes into account the exact heat gain and heat loss characteristics of a house, activating heating and cooling systems for precise time periods, thereby reducing energy consumption.

circuit See electrical terms.

circuit breaker See electrical terms.

circuit vent See plumbing terms.

circulating fan *(ventilateur de circulation, m.)* A motor-driven device used to circulate warm air from a furnace throughout a house.

circulating pump *(pompe de circulation, f.)* A motor-driven device used to circulate hot water from a boiler through a piping system in a house.

circulation See ventilation.

cistern *(citerne, f.)* A reservoir (underground or above grade) to store rainwater supply.

cladding *(parement, m.)* Any material that covers an interior or exterior wall.

clapboard *(planche à gorge, f.)* Horizontal exterior wood finish shaped or overlapped to provide a weather-proof cladding.

clay soil *(sol argileux, m.)* See soil.

cleanout (plumbing) *(regard de dégorgement, m.)* See plumbing terms.

cleanout (heating) See heating terms.

clear lumber *(bois de construction clair, m.)* Lumber which is free of knots or other blemishes.

clearance See heating terms.

clerestory *(lanterneau, m.)* An outside wall of a room or building, carried above an adjoining roof and pierced with windows. See also window types.

clinch *(river, v.)* To bend over the protruding ends of nails to resist withdrawal.

clinch nails *(clou à river, m.)* See nails, types of.

closet *(placard, m.)* Small area, usually enclosed, used for storage. See house rooms.

closet, walk-in See house rooms.

closure *(dispositif d'obturation, m.)* A device or assembly for closing an opening through a fire separation, such as a door, a shutter, wired glass or glass block, and includes all components such as hardware, closing devices, frames, and anchors.

coaxial cable *(câble coaxial, m.)* Shielded wire which typically contains a single strand copper wire core surrounded by a plastic sheath, covered in a conducting mesh and protective plastic coating. Coaxial cable is commonly used in cable television systems and has many applications in home automation.

coefficient of expansion *(coefficient de dilatation, m.)* A constant which represents the ability of a material to expand and contract due to temperature change.

coefficient of heat transmission *(coefficient de transmission de chaleur, m.)* A constant which represents the ability of a certain material to transmit heat.

coefficient of performance See heating terms.

coffered ceiling See ceiling, types.

collar tie *(entrait retroussé, m.)* A horizontal member used to provide intermediate support for opposite roof rafters, usually located in the middle third of the rafters. Also called collar beam or brace.

collector, air *(capteur à air, m.)* A solar collector that uses air as the heat transfer medium.

collector, liquid *(capteur à liquide, m.)* A solar collector that uses water or other liquid as the heat transfer medium.

collector, solar *(capteur d'énergie solaire, m.)* A device which transforms solar radiation to useable heat.

collector tilt *(inclinaison du capteur, f.)* The angle of a solar collector assembly or the roof supporting it to the horizontal.

Colombage pierroté French form of half timber framing with stone infill.

column *(poteau, m.)* A vertical member in which loads are in the direction of its longitudinal axis.

combined sewer See plumbing terms.

combined stresses *(contraintes combinées, f.)* Action of more than one force developing stresses of different character in the same member.

combustible and noncombustible material *(matériaux combustibles et incombustibles, m.)* Generally, combustible material is any material which burns, while noncombustile material does not burn. Within the range of temperatures that may occur in a building either normally or under fire conditions, materials are classified as combustible or noncombustible. The term noncombustible is generally applied to materials of construction which conform to National Standard of Canada. CAN4-S114-78, Standard Method of Test for Determination of Non-Combustibility in Building Materials. Scarborough, Ontario: Underwriters' Laboratories of Canada, 1980.

combustion *(combustion, f.)* Burning.

combustion air *(air de combustion, m.)* The air required to provide adequate oxygen for the burning of fuels in fuel-burning appliances. Some appliances use indoor air to provide this oxygen, others have a separate combustion air supply from outside.

combustion chamber *(chambre de combustion, f.)* That space in the furnace where air and fuel are mixed and ignited, and combustion is completed.

combustion liner *(chemise de la chambre de combustion, f.)* The inside of a combustion chamber, designed to withstand high temperatures.

common *(commun, adj.)* A term applied to a grade of lumber containing numerous defects which render it unsuitable for high-class finish.

common *(appareil commun, m.)* A method of laying bricks that is similar to a stretching bond but with a course of headers every fifth, sixth, or seventh course. See also stretching bond.

common rafter *(chevron commun, m.)* One of a series of rafters extending from the top of an exterior wall to the ridge of a roof.

common wall See wall, common.

communal amenity area See outdoor space. See also facilities.

composter *(composteur, m.)* A plastic or wood container with air holes, used to concentrate the natural decay of organic materials. Home vegetable waste is usually placed in an outdoor composter, along with layers of soil or manure rich in bacteria which break down the vegetable matter.

compression web-member *(membrure d'âme comprimée, f.)* See truss terminology.

concealed condensation *(condensation invisible, f.)* Condensation occurring inside an exterior wall or roof. It can cause rapid deterioration of other building components. Also referred to as interstitial condensation.

concrete *(béton, m.)* A mixture of cement, aggregate, and water.

    aerated concrete *(béton à air occlus, m.)* A lightweight concrete containing minute air-filled voids which account for a large part of its mass. It transmits less sound and heat than ordinary concrete. See also cellular concrete.

concrete (continued)

air-entrained concrete *(béton à air occlus, m.)* Concrete into which an agent has been introduced to absorb minute air bubbles that form during the mixing of concrete.

cellular concrete *(béton cellulaire, m.)* Concrete in which bubbles of air are induced, by chemical means, in the process of manufacture, thereby producing a concrete of relatively low unit weight. See also aerated concrete.

plain *(béton non armé, béton ordinaire, m.)* Concrete without reinforcement.

reinforced concrete *(béton armé, m.)* A type of construction in which the principal structural members such as floors, columns, and beams are made of concrete placed around isolated steel bars or steel meshwork in such a manner that the two materials act together in resisting force.

concrete block *(bloc de béton, m.)* A basic modular building material which is made from cement, fine aggregates, and sand. Used for structural walls and foundations.

concrete footing *(semelle de béton, f.)* The widened section at the base or bottom of a foundation wall, pier, or column.

concrete forms *(coffrage à béton, m.)* A box-like assembly of wood or metal panels into which concrete is placed to form the foundations, footings, walls, piers, or other parts of structures. Also called form work.

concrete foundation *(fondations en béton, f.)* A supporting structure made from the pouring of concrete into concrete forms. Concrete foundations usually include parging, damp-proofing and drain tiles on the exterior.

condensation *(condensation, f.)* The transformation of the vapour content of the air into water on cold surfaces.

condensing furnace See heating terms.

condominium See house types.

conduction *(conduction, f.)* Heat transfer through a material.

conductor See electrical terms.

conduit, electrical See electrical terms.

conifer, coniferous tree *(conifère, m.)* A resinous tree with cone-like fruits and needle-like or scaly leaves; generally evergreen with a few deciduous exceptions. (Not a synonym of "evergreen," which applies also to some broad-leaved plants.)

connector, box *(connecteur de boîte, m.)* A device for securing a cable by its sheath or armour, at the point it enters an enclosure such as an outlet box.

connector, wire *(serre-fils, m.)* A device that connects two or more conductors, or connects one or more conductors to a terminal point to join electrical circuits.

construction types *(constructions (types))*

adobe *(construction adobe, f.)* A type of construction in which the exterior walls are built of blocks that are made of soil mixed with straw and hardened in the sun.

block *(construction en blocs, f.)* A type of construction in which the exterior walls are bearing walls made of concrete block or structural clay tile.

construction types (continued)

brick *(construction en brique, f.)* A type of construction in which the exterior walls are bearing walls made of brick or a combination of brick and other unit masonry.

brick veneer *(construction à placage de brique, f.)* A facing of brick tied to a wood frame, concrete or masonry wall, serving as a wall covering only and carrying no structural loads.

double-wall construction *(construction à mur double, f.)* A framing technique used to increase the space for insulation by introducing a second wall that is generally non-loadbearing.

drywall *(construction à murs secs, f.)* Interior cladding with panels of gypsum board, fibre board, or plywood; a dry operation as opposed to wet plaster.

factory-built housing *(maison préfabriquée, f.)* A construction system where the complete house or portions of it are assembled in a plant, then transported to the site for final erection.

fire-resistive *(construction résistant au feu, f.)* Floors, walls, roof, etc. constructed of slow-burning or noncombustible materials recognized by building codes or local regulations to withstand collapse by fire for a stated period of time.

monolithic concrete *(construction en béton monolithe, f.)* A type of construction or process in which the concrete for the wall, floor, beams, etc. is poured in one continuous operation.

plank frame See wood framing.

post and beam See wood framing.

prefabricated *(construction préfabriquée, f.)* A type of construction so designed as to involve a minimum of assembly at the site, usually comprising a series of large wood panels or precast concrete units manufactured in a plant.

steel frame *(construction à ossature d'acier, f.)* A type of construction in which the structural parts are of steel or dependent on a steel frame for support.

wood frame *(construction à ossature de bois, f.)* A type of construction in which the structural parts are of wood or dependent upon a wood frame for support. In codes, if brick or other noncombustible material is applied to exterior walls, the classification of this type of construction is usually unchanged. See also wood framing.

contamination *(contamination, f.)* Impurities in the water supply that are serious enough to constitute an actual health hazard and render the water non-potable.

continuous caulking *(cordon de bourrage, m.)* The application of caulking as a single bead, eliminating joints and breaks. It is essential to provide a perfect seal from water and air to some components of a building such as the air barrier.

contour interval *(équidistance des courbes de niveau, f.)* The vertical distance represented by two consecutive contour lines. This interval is normally constant throughout a contour map.

contour line *(courbe de niveau, f.)* An imaginary line that joins points of equal altitude or elevation. Also called contour.

contract limit line *(limite des travaux, f.)* A line establishing the legal limit of the area inside which construction work is to be carried out.

contractor *(entrepreneur, m.)* A person or company hired for a particular job. In construction, a contractor may be hired to construct all elements of a building, but sub-contract other contractors such as electricians and plumbers, to complete specific work within the building.

control joint *(joint de rupture, m.)* A joint tooled or cut into the surface of concrete in order to control the location of cracks.

control mat *(tapis de porte automatique, m.)* A fabric or plastic pad with enclosed wiring that is placed on the floor or sidewalk inside and outside an automatic door which, when stepped upon, opens the automatic door.

controlled ventilation *(ventilation contrôlée, f.)* Ventilation brought about by mechanical means through pressure differentials induced by the operation of a fan.

convection *(convection, f.)* Transportation of heat by movement due to the ascension of air or liquid when heated and its descension when cooled. Certain types of heating systems, such as baseboard heaters, rely on convection for the distribution of heat.

convector See heating.

convenience outlet See electrical terms.

cook stove *(poêle-cuisinière, m.)* A wood burning appliance used for cooking. Some cook stoves are also capable of warming several rooms of a house and generating hot water.

cooperative See house types.

coping *(couronnement, m.)* A covering at the top of a wall exposed to the weather, designed to shed water.

corbel (masonry) *(encorbellement, m.)* A horizontal projection on the face of a wall formed by one or more courses of masonry each projecting over the course below.

core *(âme, f., noyau, m., alvéole, f.)* **(1)** The base for veneer or the piece or pieces between the surface layers. **(2)** The piece remaining after the log has been cut into veneer by the rotary process. **(3)** Preformed voids in unit masonry.

corner bead *(baguette d'angle, f.)* In plastering, a metal strip placed on external corners before plastering to protect, align, and reinforce them. In gypsum board finish, a strip of metal or wood fixed to external corners to protect them from damage.

corner boards *(boiserie cornière, f.)* A built-up wood member installed vertically on the external corners of a house or other frame structure against which the ends of the siding are butted.

cornerite *(cornerite, m.; (expression brevetée))* Metal lath cut into strips and bent to a right angle. Used in internal angles of plastered walls and ceilings as reinforcing.

cornice *(corniche, f.)* A horizontal projection at the top of a wall or column.

corrugated steel *(tôle d'acier ondulée, f.)* Sheet steel formed with parallel ripples or ridges to increase stiffness; used as a roof and wall covering and for other building purposes.

counter See truss terminology.

counter-balanced garage doors *(porte de garage à contrepoids, f.)* Garage doors designed in such a way as to open with extreme ease, using a weight or a spring to counter-balance the weight of the door.

counter brace See truss terminology.

counterflashing *(contre-solin, m.)* A flashing applied above another flashing to shed water over the top of the under flashing and to allow differential movement without damage to the flashing.

countersink *(fraisage, m.)* To make a cavity for the reception of a metal plate or the head of a screw or bolt so that it shall not project beyond the face of the work.

course *(assise, f.)* A continuous layer of bricks or masonry units in buildings; the term is also applicable to shingles.

court *(cour, f.)* An open space, unoccupied from the ground or intermediate floor to the sky, contiguous with the building and on the same lot, intended primarily for the provision of light and air, but which may serve for entrance to the building; entirely enclosed by walls or enclosed on three sides having one side partially or totally open to a street, yard, or abutting property.

coved ceiling See ceiling types.

cowl *(abat-vent, m.)* A cover, frequently louvered and either fixed or revolving, fitted to the top of a flue or vent to reduce down-draft.

crawl space *(vide sanitaire, m.)* A shallow space between the lowest floor of a house and the ground beneath.

creosote *(créosote, f.)* **(1)** An oily liquid distilled from wood or coal tar used in preserving wood in damp or wet places. **(2)** Unburned or partially unburned hydrocarbons which are byproducts of wood combustion.

cricket *(rejéteau en dos d'âne, m.)* A small roof structure at the junction of a chimney and a roof to divert rain water around the chimney. See also chimney saddle.

cross band *(placage perpendiculaire, m.)* **(1)** The layers of veneer at right angles to tile face plies. **(2)** To place layers of wood with their grains at right angles to minimize warping.

cross-bridging *(croix de Saint-André, f.)* Small wood planks or metal pegs that are inserted diagonally between adjacent floor or roof joists.

cross connections See plumbing terms.

cross grain *(veine transversale, f.)* As applied to lumber, denotes that the fibres do not run parallel to the long dimension of a piece of lumber.

cross ventilating *(ventilation transversale, f.)* The act of causing fresh air to circulate through open doors, windows, or gratings, at opposite sides of a room or space.

crushed stone *(pierre concassée, f.)* The angular particles resulting from the mechanical crushing of stone. (Not to be confused with gravel, which occurs naturally and usually has rounded surfaces).

cubical fracturing *(fissuration cubique, f.)* A condition of decayed wood in which the wood fibres are checked across the grain to form a cubical pattern on the surface of the wood.

cul-de-sac *(cul-de-sac, m.)* A short street or passageway open at one end only; also called a dead end.

culvert   See site drainage.

cupping   *(bombement, m.)* A curvature occurring in the transverse section of sawn wood.

curb   *(bordure, f.)* A low structure used to define and retain the edge of a roadway, walk, or other area.

curb box   See plumbing terms.

curb, lowered   *(bordure abaissée, f.)* A section of curb which is lowered in order to bring the level of the curb close to the level of the roadway in order to permit easier passage.

curb, rolled   *(bordure franchissable, f.)* A curb which is tapered to one side to permit the free passage of wheeled vehicles. Also called mountable curb.

curb roof or Mansard roof   See roof types.

curing (of concrete)   *(cure du béton, f.)* The maintenance of proper temperature and moisture conditions to promote the continued chemical reaction which takes place between water and cement during the setting of the cement.

curi   *(loupe, f.)* The grain pattern produced in wood when sawn at the junction of a branch and the stem of the tree.

current   See electrical terms.

curtain wall   *(mur-rideau, m.)* A thin wall whose weight is carried directly by the structural frame of the building and which supports no compressive load other than its own weight.

cut   *(déblai, m.)* The volume of earth which is removed by excavation.

cut and fill   *(déblai et remblai, m.)* The process of changing the land surface by excavating part of an area and using the resulting material to fill adjacent areas. See also fill.

cut nails   See nails, types of.

D

DDC   Acronym for direct digital control. *(commande numérique directe, f.)* An approach to home automation that relies upon dedicated wiring to receive analogue or digital signals and communicate messages to selected appliances.

D-shaped handles   *(poignées fermées, f.)* Handles for cupboards and doors that are shaped like the letter "D" for a firmer grip and better control.

dado   *(engravure, f., lambris, m.)* A rectangular groove in a board or plank.

damper   *(registre, m.)* A valve or plate for regulating draft or the flow of flue gases.

dampproof course   *(complexe d'étanchéité, m.)* A water resistant material placed just above the ground level in a brick or stone wall to prevent ground moisture from seeping up through the structure.

dampproofing   *(imperméabilisation à l'humidité, f.)* **(1)** The process of coating the outside of a foundation wall with a special preparation to resist passage of moisture through the wall. **(2)** Material used to resist the passage of moisture through concrete floor slabs and from masonry to wood.

darby float   *(lissuese, f.)* A hand float or trowel used by concrete finishers and plasterers in preliminary floating and levelling operations. Also called a derby flicker.

datum *(repère de hauteur, m.)* A reference point from which elevations and measurements are taken.

datum line *(ligne de repère de hauteur, f.)* In surveying, the base line from which all lines or levels are taken.

dead load *(charge permanente, f.)* The aggregate weight of the structural components, the fixtures and the permanently attached equipment of a building and its foundation.

deadman *(poteau d'ancrage, m.)* A piece of metal, concrete, or wood buried in ground, which is used as an anchoring device.

decay fungi *(champignon de la carie, m.)* Microbiological organisms that attack wood, including wood in buildings, as a source of nutrient.

deciduous *(à feuilles caduques, adj.)* Describes woody plants which lose their leaves each year.

deck *(plate-forme, f., terrasse en bois, f.)* An elevated, unroofed platform attached to a dwelling. Generally constructed of wood members spaced to permit the passage of water between them.

deck, roof See roof types.

defect *(vice, m.)* A fault or irregularity in lumber which detracts from utility, durability, strength, or appearance.

deflection *(flèche, f.)* A deviation or turning aside from a set line; bending of a beam or any part of a structure under an applied load.

deformation *(déformation, f.)* Alterations in forms which a structure undergoes when subjected to the action of weight or load.

deformed bar *(barre à haute adhérence, f.)* Reinforcing bars made in irregular shapes to produce a better bond between the bars and concrete.

degree day *(degré-jour, m.)* A daily measure of difference between the average outside temperature and 18°C. The seasonal sum of degree days below 18°C is used in calculating heating requirements.

dehumidify *(déshumidifier, v.)* To reduce, by any process, the quantity of water vapour or moisture content in the air of a room.

dehumidistat *(déshumidistat, m.)* A device that senses the level of humidity in the home. If too high or low, the humidity is adjusted accordingly, using the supply of ventilation and air.

delayed action solenoid valve See heating terms.

densification *(densification, f.)* An approach to urban planning and development that argues against the absorption of farm land and green fields on the outskirts of cities, and for growth to be directed towards more population intensive solutions, such as adding apartments to small commercial buildings and encouraging creative residential and mixed use construction projects in the urban core.

densified pellet technology *(granule, f.)* The use of pellets of dried ground wood or other biomass waste as a form of fuel in a wood burning appliance. The pellets normally burn more cleanly than natural firewood. Also see pellet stove.

depressurization *(dépressurisation, f.)* The condition of a house or part of a house when air pressure inside is less than outdoor air pressure. Commonly caused by kitchen and bathroom exhaust fans.

desiccant *(siccatif, m.)* An agent that removes moisture from air or materials.

design heat losses *(déperdition de chaleur de calcul, f.)* The total, predicted, envelope heat losses over the heating season for a particular house design in a particular climate.

detached house See house types.

dew point *(point de rosée, m.)* The temperature at which a given air/water vapour mixture is saturated with water vapour (i.e., 100% relative humidity). If air is in contact with a surface below this temperature, condensation will form on the surface.

diagonal ties *(écharpes, f.)* **(1)** Braces or ties which help stiffen a roof truss. **(2)** Braces attached to an angle to tie framing members together.

dielectric coupling See plumbing terms.

diffusion (water-vapour diffusion) *(diffusion de vapeur, f.)* The movement of water vapour through materials (including air) and caused by a difference in vapour pressure. It is independent of air movement.

dilution air See heating terms.

dimension stock *(bois de dimension, m.)* Dressed lumber cut to standard sizes which are readily available at local lumber dealers.

dinette See house rooms.

dining room See house rooms.

dip See plumbing terms.

direct current See electrical terms.

direct gain *(système naturel du type fenêtres, m.)* A term referring to a type of solar heating system where the solar collection area is an integral part of the building's usable space.

direct load control *(régulation directe, f.)* The control of a residential appliance by a power utility. For example, the remote turning off of a water heater by the utility company when a sensor on the water heater has determined a certain interior tank temperature has been reached. Direct load control can be achieved through the use of simple timers or sophisticated two-way communications systems.

direct siphonage See plumbing terms.

direct vent appliance *(appareil à combustion optimisée, m.)* An appliance constructed so that all the combustion air is supplied directly from, and the products of combustion are vented directly to, outdoors, by independent enclosed passageways connected directly to the appliance. Also called a sealed combustion system appliance.

distributed load *(charge distribuée, f.)* In building, a load spread over an entire surface or along the length of a beam.

distribution See ventilation.

distribution box *(boîte de distribution, f.)* See electrical terms.

distribution pipe See plumbing terms.

door casing *(encadrement de porte, m.)* The finishing material around a door opening.

door jamb *(chambranle de porte, m.)* Sides of a frame set in a wall or partition on which a door is hung.

door sill *(seuil de porte, m.)* A horizontal member forming the bottom of an outside door frame over which the door closes.

door stop *(butoir de porte, m.)* A device fitted to a door, or on the floor or wall near a door, to hold it open as far as may be required, or to prevent the door from being opened beyond a certain amount; the strip against which a door closes on the face of a door frame.

dormer *(lucarne, f.)* Framing which projects from a sloping roof, providing an internal recess in the roof space.

dormer window See window terminology.

double glazing *(double vitrage, m.)* Two panes of glass in a door or window, with an air space between the panes. They may be sealed hermetically as a single unit or each pane may be installed separately in the door or window sash.

double header *(chevêtre jumelé, m.)* A structural member made by nailing or bolting two joists together for use where extra strength is required in the header, as at stair openings.

double-hung window See window terminology.

double shell house *(maison à double paroi, f.)* A method of house building that creates a space in the wall for a continuous convection current between exterior and interior house envelopes.

double-wall flue pipe *(conduit de fumée doublé, m.)* A chimney flue made with a metal inner liner and a sealed or ventilated outer shell, used on wood burning appliances.

dovetailing See joints.

dowel *(goujon, m.)* A pin of wood or metal used to hold or strengthen two pieces of timber where they join; a pin or tenon fitting into a corresponding hole serving to fasten two pieces of wood together.

down-draft *(contre-tirage, m.)* A draft created in a chimney when air currents enter at the top and travel down; sometimes caused by not carrying the chimney high enough above the ridge of the roof.

downsize See heating terms.

downspout *(descente pluviale, f.)* A pipe which carries water from the eavestrough to the ground or the storm drainage system.

draft *(tirage, m.)* The pressure difference existing between an appliance or any component part and the atmosphere which causes a continuous flow of air and products of combustion through the gas passages of the appliance to the atmosphere.

draft hood See heating terms.

draft stop *(coupe-feu, m.)* An obstruction placed in a concealed space to block the passage of flame or air currents upwards or across a building. Also called a fire stop.

drain   See plumbing terms.

drainage   See site drainage.

drainage pipe   See plumbing terms.

drainage piping   See plumbing terms.

drainage swale   *(rigole de drainage, f.)* A small channel that is usually grassed and is wider than deep. It is used for the removal of surface water from a site by natural run-off.

drainage system   See plumbing terms.

drainage tile   *(drain français ou de semelle, m.)* Pipe laid in gravel around the footings of a building to drain sub-surface water away from the foundation walls.

dress   *(corroyer, v.)* To plane one or more sides of a piece of sawn lumber.

dressing   *(équarrissage, m.)* The operation of squaring or smoothing stones or lumber for building purposes.

drier   See paint.

drip   *(larmier, m.)* A construction member, wood or metal, which projects to throw off rain water. A groove on the underside of a projecting part, such as a sill, serving the purpose.

drip leg   See plumbing terms: relief pipe.

drip line   *(limite de feuillage, f.)* A line projected downwards which corresponds to the limit of a tree's foliage.

drip mould   *(réjeteau, m.)* A projecting moulding arranged to throw off rain water from the face of a wall.

driveway   See outdoor spaces.

dropped ceiling   *(faux plafond, m.)* A ceiling constructed immediately below the roof or existing ceiling, allowing for mechanical equipment, insulation and a continuous air and vapour barrier.

drop siding   *(bardage à mi-bois, m.)* Weather-boarding which is rabbeted and overlapped.

dry-kiln   See kiln.

dry rot   *(pourriture sèche, f.)* A decay of timber due to the attack of certain fungi.

dry-stone wall   *(mur de pierres sèches, m.)* A wall made of stone laid without mortar, normally used as a low retaining wall.

drywall   *(panneau mural sec, m.)* Gypsum board, fibre board or plywood that is used as interior cladding.

drywall compound   *(pâte à jointoyer, f.)* A type of plaster used to seal the joints between sheets of drywall.

drywall construction   *(construction à murs secs, f.)* See construction types.

drywall finish   *(finition à murs secs, m.)* Interior wall and ceiling finish other than plaster - e.g. gypsum board, fibre-board panels, plywood, etc. Often used interchangeably with gypsum board.

dry well   See plumbing terms.

dual setting thermostat   *(thermostat à deux réglages, m.)* A thermostat which offers two temperature settings, usually for day and night. Also called night setback.

duct *(conduits d'air, m.)* In building construction, usually a metal pipe, round or rectangular in shape, for distributing air in heating and ventilating systems.

ductless furnace See heating terms.

duct tape *(ruban à conduits, m.)* Vinyl and foil tapes used to seal around the seams of ductwork to temporarily reduce air leakage.

duel venting See plumbing terms.

duplex See house types.

dust mite *(acarien de la poussière, m.)* A microscopic animal that lives on skin flakes in house dust.

dwarf wall or partition See partition.

dwelling, multiple *(logement collectif, m.)* Any building or part thereof designed, intended, or used for residential occupancy consisting of more than two units. It can take the form of apartment houses, terraces, rows, and group houses.

dwelling unit *(logement, m.)* One or more rooms used or intended for the domestic use of one or more individuals living as a single housekeeping unit, with cooking, eating, living, sleeping, and sanitary facilities.

E

ECM Acronym for electrically commutated motors. *(No French equivalent)* Motors which use electronics instead of brushes to sense the position of the rotor. Their speed can be easily controlled with electronics.

EIFS Acronym for exterior insulation finish systems. *(PEI Parement extérieur isolant)* Generic description of a composite type of building cladding that consists mainly of externally applied rigid insulation board, glass fibre reinforcing mesh and synthetic stucco.

ELA See equivalent leakage area.

EMC See equilibrium moisture content.

EMCS Acronym for Energy Management Control System. *(SCSCE Système de commande et de surveillance de la consommation d'énergie)* A system that integrates humidity control, air quality control, temperature setting, and time-of-day energy use to produce high levels of occupant comfort and optimize energy use.

ER See window terminology.

ESCO See energy savings company.

earth *(terre, f.)* Materials other than rock, resulting from the disintegration of rock masses, are broadly classed as earth. Note: the word soil, when used to designate any earthy material that is not rock, is a misnomer, in that the idea of fertility, or the lack of it, is conveyed when the word soil is used. See also soil.

earthwork *(terrassement, m.)* The moving of surface materials to create a change of landform during site construction.

easement *(servitude, f.)* Part of a property that is legally accessible to a person or public authority other than the owner, for a right-of-way or the passage of services.

eave *(avant-toit, m.)* The part of a roof which projects beyond the face of the wall.

eave soffit *(sous-face de débord de toit, f.)* The under surface of the eave.

eavestrough *(gouttière de débord de toit, f.)* A trough fixed to an eave to collect and carry away the run-off from the roof. Also called gutter.

edge grain *(débit sur maille, m.)* Lumber that is sawn along the radius of the annual rings or at an angle less than 45° to the radius; synonymous with quarter sawn.

edge nails *(clouage en biais à la rive, m.)* Blind or secret nailing, a method used in laying and nailing hardwood flooring.

edging *(bordure, f.)* A linear barrier, often of paving stone, between two surface materials; commonly used between a lawn and gravel.

efflorescence *(efflorescence, f.)* Formation of a white crystalline deposit on the face of masonry walls.

egress *(sortie, f.)* An outlet; a place of exit.

electric boiler See heating terms.

electric box air barrier *(pare-air de boîte d'électricité, m.)* Plastic boxes placed around electrical outlet and switch boxes before installation, equipped with a flange for sealing to the main air barrier, and acting as vapour barriers.

electric furnace See heating terms.

electric ignition See heating terms.

electrical terms *(Électricité, terminologie)*

    alternating current *(courant alternatif, m.)* A flow of current which constantly changes direction at a fixed rate.

    ampere *(ampère, m.)* The unit of electrical current equivalent to the steady current produced by one volt applied across a resistance of one ohm.

    ampacity *(courant admissible, m.)* The current-carrying capacity of electric conductors expressed in amperes.

    branch circuit *(circuit de dérivation, m.)* The circuit conductors between the final overcurrent devices (fuses) protecting the circuit, outlets and fixtures.

    cable *(câble, m.)* A bundle of insulated wire to carry an electrical current.

    cable, armoured *(câble armé, m.)* Insulated wire having additional flexible metallic protective sheathing — often referred to as BX cable.

    ceiling outlet *(sortie électrique au plafond, f.)* An outlet for a ceiling lighting fixture.

    circuit *(circuit, m.)* Continuous conducting path through which current flows.

    circuit breaker *(disjoncteur, m.)* An electromechanical device designed to open a current-carrying circuit, under overload or short circuit conditions, without injury to the device; serves the same purpose as a fuse, i.e. to prevent overheating in a circuit through overloading. Unlike a fuse, a circuit breaker can be reset, rather than replaced.

    conductor *(conducteur, m.)* A wire, cable or other form of metal of low resistance, capable of conducting or transmitting electrical current from one piece of electrical equipment to another, or to ground.

    conduit, electrical *(conduit électrique, m.)* A protective pipe-like covering for electrical wiring.

electrical terms (continued)

convenience outlet *(prise confort, f.)* An outlet into which may be plugged portable equipment, such as lamps or electrically operated equipment.

current *(courant, m.)* A flow of electricity.

direct current *(courant continu, m.)* A flow of current constantly in one direction.

distribution box *(boîte de distribution, f.)* A protected housing which serves as the transition point between the service entrance and the distribution circuits and contains the overcurrent devices (fuses or breakers) that protect each circuit.

feeder *(artère, f.)* A conductor that transmits electrical energy from a service supply, transformer, switchboard, distribution centre, generator or other source to branch circuit overcurrent devices.

fuse *(fusible, m.)* A device capable of automatically opening an electric circuit under predetermined overload or short-circuit conditions by fusing or melting; an overcurrent device.

fuse rejecters *(rondelle de rejet, f.)* A plastic disc that fits into the base of a fuse socket and prevents the installation of a fuse of higher amperage than was intended for the circuit.

ground *(terre, f.)* A connection to earth by means of a conductor with a very low impedance.

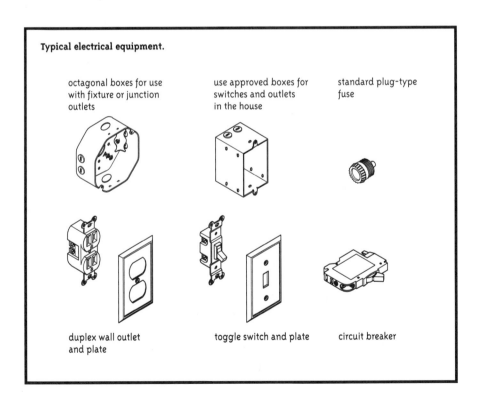

Typical electrical equipment.

octagonal boxes for use with fixture or junction outlets

use approved boxes for switches and outlets in the house

standard plug-type fuse

duplex wall outlet and plate

toggle switch and plate

circuit breaker

electrical terms (continued)

ground electrode *(électrode de masse, f.)* A heavy conductor or network of conductors, usually buried in the earth, to provide a conducting connection between an electrical circuit or equipment and earth.

ground fault circuit interrupter *(disjoncteur différentiel, m.)* A device designed to interrupt, almost instantaneously, an accidental connection between a live part of an electrical system and ground (a short circuit or a shock) when the current exceeds a very small predetermined value. This device will react to a dangerous situation before a fuse or circuit breaker, and before a human can be harmed by the shock.

grounding system *(installation de mise à la terre, f.)* All conductors, clamps, ground clips, ground plates or pipes and ground electrodes by which the electrical installation is grounded.

hot bar *(barre collectrice thermique, f.)* Metallic bar located in the distribution box which serves as a transition between the power carrying service line and the fuse or circuit rake.

hot line *(conducteur actif, m.)* A power carrying wire, usually black or red; an extension of the input power lines from the utility. Hot lines are protected by fuses or circuit breakers.

impedance *(impédance, f.)* The quantity which determines the amplitude of the current for a given voltage.

insulate *(isoler, v.)* To separate from other conducting surfaces by a material or air space that resists the passage of current.

insulation, electrical *(isolant électrique, m.)* Non-conducting covering applied to wire or equipment to prevent short circuiting.

jump wire *(fil-jarretière, m.)* A grounding wire that bridges the water meter to the ground electrode of street side plumbing when the electrical system has been grounded to the house side of the plumbing system.

kilowatt hour *(kilowatt-heure, m.)* A unit of measurement of the consumption of electric energy at a fixed rate for 1 hour; specifically, the use of 1000 watts for 1 hour. (Metric replacement of kWh is MJ. 1kWh = 3.6 MJ.)

knob-and-tube wiring *(canalisation électrique à isolateurs et tubulures, f.)* Very old wiring with single insulated wires strung between porcelain knobs and through porcelain tubes.

load miser *(contrôleur de charge, m.)* An overload device that allows two demand loads on one set of fuses; usually used where the service is not of adequate size to supply two large applicances simultaneously.

low melting point fuse *(fusible à bas point de fusion, m.)* A fuse designed to blow, due to heat build-up, in addition to excessive current flowing. Therefore, these fuses can trip when less than their rated current is flowing if sufficient heat is generated. Also called a Type P fuse.

main switch *(interrupteur général, m.)* A two-pole switch capable of cutting off all the electricity in a system. It is installed between the meter and distribution box, or ahead of the meter.

meter *(compteur, m.)* A device used for recording consumption of electricity.

electrical terms (continued)

meter socket *(embase, f.)* The socket that contains the electrical connections on both sides of the meter and into which the meter is installed.

neutral block *(fils compensateurs, m.)* A metallic block of wire connectors located within the distribution box which serves as a transition between the service entrance neutral wire and the white return wires of the distribution system.

ohm *(ohm, m.)* A unit of electrical resistance defined as the resistance between two points of a conductor when a constant application of one volt produces a current of one ampere.

outlet *(prise de courant, f.)* A device on the wiring system at which current is taken to supply fixtures or applicances.

overload device *(dispositif de protection contre les surcharges, m.)* Any device affording protection from excess current, but not necessarily short circuit protection, and capable of automatically opening an electric circuit either by fusing of metal or by electromechanical means.

overloading *(surcharge, f.)* The surcharge of a circuit beyond the capacity of its conductors.

panelboard *(panneau de distribution, m.)* A centre for controlling a number of circuits by means of fuses or circuit breakers, usually contained in a metal cabinet. Switches are sometimes added to control each circuit.

panel schedule *(diagramme, m.)* A diagram of the arrangement of fuses or breakers, identifying each circuit; usually found on the door to the panel where the circuit breakers or fuses are kept.

power *(puissance, f.)* The amount of energy expended or produced in a given time; measured in watts.

power circuit *(circuit de puissance, m.)* A circuit transmitting electric energy to a motor or to a heating unit too large to be served by an ordinary circuit.

radio outlet *(branchement de radio, m.)* An outlet with an aerial and ground for the use of a radio connected to it. Radio outlets are no longer in use.

receptacle *(prise de courant femelle, f.)* A contact device installed at the outlet into which electric cords can be plugged.

safety switch *(interrupteur de sécurité, m.)* A fused interrupter which will cut off all electricity to a major appliance.

service box *(coffret de branchement, m.)* An assembly consisting of a metal box or cabinet that can be locked or sealed, containing either fuses or circuit breakers.

service head *(caisse de tête, f.)* A weatherproof device through which the service lines enter the service mast or conduit.

service lines *(branchements, m.)* The incoming power lines to the distribution box.

service mast *(mât de service, m.)* A conduit extension used to raise the service head to a height adequate to assure proper clearance for overhead service lines.

short circuit *(court-circuit, m.)* An accidental connection of two sides of a circuit through which nearly all the current will flow. Also called short.

electrical terms (continued)

special purpose outlet *(prise de courant spéciale, f.)* An outlet used for purposes other than ordinary lighting and power, usually fused separately. Most commonly used for ranges or clothes dryers.

stress strap *(courroie de sécurité, f.)* A clamp that holds an electrical cable firmly to an appliance to prevent any chance of the connector being pulled out under stress.

switch *(interrupteur, m.)* A device for making, breaking or changing connections in a circuit.

three-way switch *(interrupteur tripolaire, m.)* A switch designed to operate in conjunction with a similar switch to control one outlet or light fixture from either of two points. Commonly used at opposite ends of stairs and hallways.

time delay fuse *(fusible à action différée, m.)* An overcurrent device which allows a large surge current for a short period of time but will open if current demand is over its predetermined smaller rating on a continuous basis; used primarily to protect electric motor circuits, large appliances and stationary power tools. Also called a Type D fuse.

transformer *(transformateur, m.)* A device for changing the voltage characteristics of a current supply.

Type D fuse See time delay fuse.

Type P fuse See low melting point fuse.

volt *(volt, m.)* A unit of electromotive force (ie. The force that tends to cause movement of electricity around an electric circuit) or potential difference; equal to the electromagnetic field that causes a current of one ampere to flow through a conductor with a resistance of one ohm.

voltage *(voltage, m.)* A measure of electric pressure between any two wires of an electric circuit.

watt *(watt, m.)* A unit of measurement of electric power; the energy expended per second by an electric current of one ampere flowing through a conductor the ends of which are maintained at a potential difference of one volt.

electrical outlet and lighting gaskets *(joint d'étanchéité pour prises et lampes électriques, m.)* Foam gaskets designed to fit behind the cover plates of electrical receptacles, switches and lighting mounts, reducing air leakage into walls and attics.

electrode filter *(filtre à électrodes, m.)* A device which uses two electrodes to control bacteria in water. A mild electrical current is passed between two bars of different metals to kill micro-organisms in water. A copper electrode eliminates algae and a silver electrode kills bacteria. Electrode filters are used where it is desirable to use as few water treatment chemicals as possible.

electrolysis *(électrolyse, f.)* An electrochemical reaction between two dissimilar metals, such as copper and galvanized steel, causing corrsion of a joint where the two materials are in contact with each other.

electromagnetic radiation *(radiation électromagnétique, f.)* Radiation produced by the electromagnetic field (EMF) generated artificially by electric currents and naturally by the earth (emanating from the ground).

electrostatic air filtration *(filtration d'air électrostatique, f.)* The use of electronic air cleaners or plastic fibres to clean air by attracting particles with an electric charge.

elevation *(élévation, f., niveau, m.)* The vertical distance between a point and a reference point.

elevator *(ascenseur, m.)* A lifting device in which a platform can be moved up or down a shaft, either by hoists from above or a hydraulic cylinder below.

enamel *(émail, m.)* See paint.

enclosed stairway See stairway types.

end grain *(veine d'extrémité, m.)* The face of a piece of lumber which is exposed when the fibres are cut transversely.

end matched *(bout embouveté, m.)* Lumber with tongued-and-grooved ends.

end thrust *(poussée d'extrémité, f.)* A pressure exerted in the direction of the ends of a structural member, such as a girder, beam, truss, or rafter.

energy retrofit *(amélioration éconergétique, m.)* A process through which the energy consumption of an existing building or home is reduced. Properly executed retrofits consider building as a system approaches that examine the reductions that are made possible by retrofitting related systems in combination. For example, when old heating systems are replaced, the building envelope should be assessed. A smaller, more efficient furnace might be installed if the air leaks and insulation levels are addressed.

energy savings company (ESCO) *(entreprise de services éconergétiques ESO)* Businesses which will undertake energy retrofits of any structure at little or no cost to the owner. In exchange, the esco will be paid through the energy and water savings, which over time, should far exceed the initial cost of retrofit. Payback periods are an essential consideration of escos.

English bond *(appareil anglais, m.)* The form of masonry bond in which each course is alternately composed entirely of headers or of stretchers.

ensuite *(salle de bains communicante, f.)* A private room attached to another room, e.g., an ensuite bathroom attached to a bedroom.

envelope *(enveloppe, f.)* The exterior surface of a building that separates the indoor heated air from outdoor air. It includes all external additions, e.g., chimneys, bay windows, etc.

environmental hypersensitivity *(hypersensibilité environnementale, f.)* A condition in which a person may suffer allergy-like reactions to substances in the air of a building.

equilibrium moisture content (EMC) *(équilibre hygrométrique, m.)* The moisture content at which wood neither gains nor loses moisture to the air around it when the air is at a constant relative humidity.

equivalent leakage area (ELA) *(surface équivalente de fuite, f.)* An estimate of the total area of all the unintentional openings in a building envelope, generally expressed in square centimetres or square inches.

erosion *(érosion, f.)* The uncontrolled detachment and removal of soil particles by the action of water, wind, or gravity.

escutcheon *(cache-entrée, m.)* A perforated plate around an opening, such as a keyhole plate or the plate to which a door knob is attached.

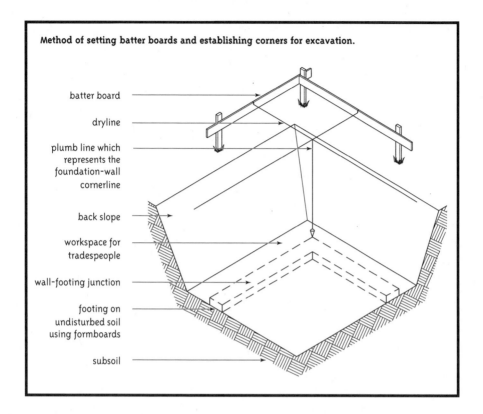

Method of setting batter boards and establishing corners for excavation.

batter board

dryline

plumb line which represents the foundation-wall cornerline

back slope

workspace for tradespeople

wall-footing junction

footing on undisturbed soil using formboards

subsoil

excavate *(creuser, v.)* To dig or scoop out earth as for a foundation.

exfiltration *(exfiltration, f.)* The uncontrolled escape of air through cracks and pores of a building.

exhaust shaft *(puits d'extraction, m.)* A ventilating passage used to convey air away from rooms.

exit *(issue, f.)* That part of a means of egress that leads from the floor area it serves, including any doorway leading directly from a floor area, to another floor area, to a public thoroughfare, or to an open space.

exit, access to *(accès à l'issue, m.)* That part of a means of egress within a floor area that provides access to an exit serving the floor area.

exit, horizontal *(issue horizontale, f.)* The connection by a bridge, balcony, vestibule, or doorway of two floor areas at substantially the same level; such floor areas being located either in different buildings or located in the same building and fully separated from each other by a firewall.

exotic species *(espèce exotique ou introduite, f.)* A plant or animal that is not native but is introduced to the site in which it is found; opposite of native or indigenous species.

expanded metal *(métal expansé, m.)* A metal network formed by stamping or cutting sheet-metal and stretching it to form open meshes. It is used as reinforcing in concrete construction and as lath for plastering and stucco.

expanded polystyrene *(polystyrène expansé, m.)* A cladding produced by bonding coarse beads into rigid foam plastic boards; often called "bead board".

expansion bolts *(boulons à expansion, m.)* Fasteners commonly used for bolting wood or iron to concrete or masonry, and are able to hold the connection despite the expansion or contraction of the wood or iron.

expansion joint See joints.

expansive soils *(sol gonflant, m.)* Fine-grained soils such as clay, silt and fine sand which are frost-susceptible and therefore more subject to frost heaving.

expansion tank *(réservoir de dilatation, m.)* In a hot-water system, a tank designed to allow expansion of the water on heating.

exterior trim *(boiserie extérieure, f.)* Exterior mouldings and members used to cover unprotected edges or joints of exterior finish.

extrados *(extrados, m.)* The upper curved line of an arch.

extruded polystyrene *(polystyrène extrudé, m.)* A foam plastic board with fine, closed cells containing a mixture of air and high-molecular weight gases (often fluorocarbons) used as an insulation material.

F

ft.b.m.   See board foot.

façade   *(façade, f.)* The whole exterior side of a building that can be seen at one view; the principal front.

face nailing *(clouage de face, m.)* Fastening a member by driving nails through it at right angles to its exposed surface.

facer board *(bordure de pignon, f.)* The board under the verge of gables, sometimes moulded; sometimes referred to as verge board. See also barge board.

face side *(côté de la face, m.)* That side of a piece of lumber or a panel which shows the best quality.

facilities *(services, m.)*

   community facilities *(services communautaires, m.)* Common, social, recreational, or convenience facilities, such as social halls, public utilities, central heating, parks, private roads, playgrounds, and accommodation for them.

   living facilities *(commodités domiciliaires, f.)* Those provisions for living, sleeping, eating, cooking, and sanitation ordinarily considered as part of a permanent abode.

facing   *(revêtement, m.)* The external layer of a wall, which is visible and exposed to the weather, supported by a structural wall behind.

factor of safety *(facteur de sécurité, m.)* In design, the ratio allowed for between the breaking load on a member or structure, and the safe permissible load on it.

factory-built chimney See chimney, types.

factory-built housing See construction types.

false ceiling *(faux-plafond, m.)* A suspended ceiling formed to provide covered accommodation for wires, conduits, pipe ducts, etc.

family room See house rooms.

fan depressurization *(dépressurisation par ventilateur, f.)* A process by which a large fan is used to exhaust air from a building in order to create a pressure difference across the building envelope. An analysis of the flow rate through the fan at different pressure differences provides a measurement of airtightness.

fasciaboard *(bordure d'avant-toit, f.)* A finish member around the face of eaves and roof projections.

faucet See plumbing terms.

feather edge *(planche à clin, f.)* An exterior wood siding applied horizontally, thinner on one edge than the other.

feathering *(amincissement, m.)* Reducing gradually to a very thin edge.

feeder See electrical terms.

felt paper *(papier feutré, m.)* A building paper of strong, tough paper base saturated with hot bitumen and rolled smooth; used under roofing and siding materials as a protection against moisture and air infiltration.

fence *(clôture, f.)* A man-made barrier used to define or enclose an area.

fenestration *(fenêtrage, m.)* The distribution or arrangement of windows, doors, and ornamental trim.

fertilizer *(fertilisant, engrais, m.)* An artificial or natural substance added to the soil to provide one or more of the nutrients essential to the growth of plants; the principal ones being nitrogen, phosphorus, and potassium.

fibreboard *(carton-fibre, m.)* An insulating lath or wallboard of compressed wood fibres.

fibreboard, hard-pressed *(carton-fibre comprimé, m.)* A material manufactured of wood fibres and used for wall cladding.

fibreglass *(fibre de verre, f.)* (1) A compound consisting of glass fibres drawn or blown directly from a glass melt; commonly used in a composite with a plastic polymer. (2) See glass fibre.

fibre optics *(fibres optiques, f.)* Hair-thin fibres which offer the ability to transmit audio, video, and data information as coded light pulses. Their use in telephone lines has made possible the use of facsimile and modem technology.

fibre saturation point *(point de saturation des fibres, m.)* That point reached in seasoning lumber when all the free water has been driven off, leaving water only in the cell walls; the point at which lumber begins to shrink (approximately 25 to 30 per cent moisture content).

fill *(remblai, m.)* Earth, soil, or other material used to alter the existing topographic relief of an area. See also cut and fill.

filler See paint.

filter *(filtre, m.)* A device that removes impurities from liquids or gases. Filters may be used in the plumbing system to purify the domestic water supply and in the heating system to protect the furnace fan from debris. Upgraded heating system filters will remove some airborne particulates from the air circulated around the house.

fin tubes *(tuyau à ailettes, m.)* A network of tubes used to increase the internal surface area in an assembly with heat exchanger properties. Fin tubes can be found, for example, in the sub-floor assembly of a radiant heating floor through which a warm fluid flows.

fine grain *(veine fine, f.)* Describes wood with narrow annual rings.

finial *(faîteau, m.)* An ornament, often long and narrow, set at the peak of a gable.

finished size *(dimensions finies, f.)* The overall measurements of any object completely finished and ready for use.

finish grading *(régalage, nivellement final, m.)* The final surface adjustments made to a site after construction of buildings and other facilities. Usually applies to manual placing and raking of topsoil.

fire barriers *(éléments coupe-feu, m.)* Fire resistant walls, doors, and similar construction to prevent spread of a fire in a building. See also fire stop.

fire brick *(brique réfractaire, f.)* A brick made with high heat-resisting clay, used to line some fireplaces, furnaces and chimneys.

fire clay *(argile réfractaire, f.)* A clay of high heat-resisting qualities used to make fire brick and the mortar in which fire brick is laid.

fire compartment *(compartiment coupe-feu, m.)* An enclosed interior space in a building that is separated from all other parts of the building by enclosing construction providing a fire separation having a required fire resistance rating.

fire damper *(registre coupe-feu, m.)* A method of closure which consists of a normal damper installed in an air distribution system or in a wall or floor assembly, which is held open but designed to close automatically in the event of a fire to maintain the integrity of the fire separation.

fire door *(porte coupe-feu, f.)* A point of entrance or egress which opens and shuts with a slab manufactured to be fire resistant.

fire door types *(genres de portes coupe-feu, m.)*

> **heat-actuated fire door** *(porte coupe-feu commandée par la chaleur, f.)* One in which a mechanism operates under the action of heat causing the door to close automatically.

> **self-closing fire door** *(porte coupe-feu à fermeture automatique, f.)* A fire door normally closed and designed to close automatically upon being opened.

fire load *(charge combustible, f.)* As applied to an occupancy, means the combustible contents of a room or floor area expressed in terms of the average weight of combustible materials per square metre, from which the potential heat liberation may be calculated on the calorific value of the materials and includes the furnishings, finished floor, wall and ceiling finishes, trim, and temporary and movable partitions.

fire partition See partition.

fireplace *(foyer, m.)* A wood or gas burning appliance that is normally built into the structure of the house. Traditional fireplaces are usually ineffective for home heating, generally losing more heat than they generate; used mainly for fire viewing.

fireplace inserts *(poêle encastrable, m.)* A manufactured, generally metal firebox and accessories that fit into a masonry fireplace opening.

fire-protection rating *(degré pare-flammes, m.)* The time in hours or fractions or hours that a closure, window assembly or glass block assembly will withstand the passage of flame when exposed to fire under specified test and performance criteria.

fire resistance rating *(degré de résistance au feu, m.)* The time in hours or fractions of hours that a material or assembly of materials will withstand the passage of flame and the transmission of heat when exposed to fire under specified conditions of test and performance criteria.

fire-resistive construction See construction types.

fire separation *(séparation coupe-feu, f.)* A construction assembly that acts as a barrier against the spread of fire, which may or may not be required to have a fire-resistance rating.

fire stop *(coupe-feu, m.)* A draft-tight barrier within or between construction assemblies that acts to retard the passage of smoke and flame.

firewall *(mur coupe-feu, m.)* A wall of noncombustible construction, which subdivides a building into limited fire areas or separates adjoining buildings so as to resist the spread of fire and which has a fire-resistance rating as prescribed and structural stability to remain intact under fire conditions for the required fire-rated time.

fire window See window types.

fixed sash See sash types.

fixture See plumbing terms.

fixture trap See plumbing terms.

flag stones *(dalles, f.)* Flat stones, usually from 25-75 mm thick, used for floors, pavement, or sidewalks.

flame-spread rating *(indice de propagation des flammes, f.)* The measurement of flame spread on the surface of a material or an assembly of materials as determined in a standard fire test.

flange *(aile, semelle, f.)* **(1)** A projecting edge, rib, or rim. **(2)** The top and bottom of I-beams and channels.

flapper *(clapet, m.)* In a toilet, a rubber plate that lifts during flushing to allow water to flow out of the tank and into the bowl; when the tank refills, the flapper drops into the valve seat and seals.

flashing *(solin, m.)* Sheet metal or other material used in roof and wall construction to shed water.

flat grain *(débit en plot, m.)* Plain-sawn or sawn tangential to the annual rings, as opposed to edge grain or quarter-sawn.

flat roof See roof types.

flat slab *(dalle sans nervure, f., plancher-dalle, m.)* A concrete slab reinforced in two or more directions, without beams or girders except wall or trimmer beams, from which loads are transferred to supporting columns.

Flemish bond *(appareil flamand, m.)* In masonry, a bond consisting of alternate headers and stretchers in every course, each header being placed in the middle of the stretchers, in the courses above and below.

flight *(volée d'escalier, f.)* A series of steps between floors or landings.

float finish *(fini aplani, m.)* A type of finish on concrete or plaster.

floating *(aplanissement, m.)* The equal spreading of plaster or concrete by means of a board called a float.

floor drain *(siphon de sol, m.)* A waste water outlet and trap usually placed at a low point in a sloping concrete floor.

flooring *(revêtement de sol, m.)* Material used in the construction of floors. The surface material is known as finished flooring while the base material is called sub-flooring.

floor joist See joists.

flue See chimney flue.

flue collar *(buse, f.)* That portion of an appliance designed for the attachment of a draft hood, vent connector or venting system.

flue damper, automatic *(registre de tirage clapet, m.)* A damper added to a flue pipe downstream of a furnace or boiler and connected with automatic controls to the burner, in order to reduce heat loss when the heating device is not operating.

flue lining See chimney flue and tile.

flue pipe *(carneau, m., conduit de fumée, m.)* The pipe conducting combustion products from the furnace or boiler to the chimney.

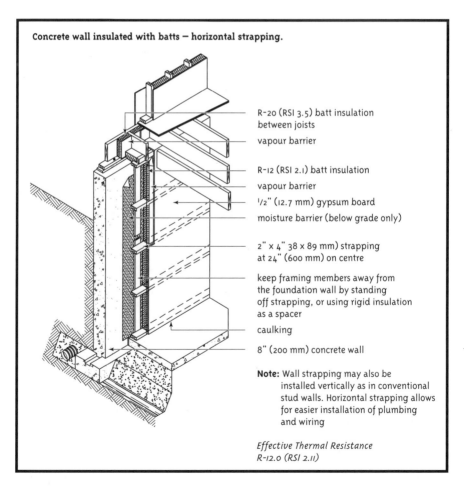

Concrete wall insulated with batts — horizontal strapping.

R-20 (RSI 3.5) batt insulation between joists

vapour barrier

R-12 (RSI 2.1) batt insulation

vapour barrier

¹/₂" (12.7 mm) gypsum board

moisture barrier (below grade only)

2" x 4" 38 x 89 mm) strapping at 24" (600 mm) on centre

keep framing members away from the foundation wall by standing off strapping, or using rigid insulation as a spacer

caulking

8" (200 mm) concrete wall

Note: Wall strapping may also be installed vertically as in conventional stud walls. Horizontal strapping allows for easier installation of plumbing and wiring

Effective Thermal Resistance R-12.0 (RSI 2.11)

flute *(cannelure, f.)* A rounded groove on a column or pilaster.

footing *(semelle, f.)* The widened section, usually concrete, at the base or bottom of a foundation wall, pier, or column.

forced warm air heating See heating.

formaldehyde *(formaldéhyde, m.)* A common toxic gas which can be released by certain glues, insulation, furnishings, plastics and curing agents.

form work See concrete forms.

foundation *(fondations, f.)* The lower portion of a structure, usually concrete or masonry, including the footings, which transfers the weight of, and loads on the structure to the ground.

foundation drain See plumbing terms.

foyer *(hall d'entrée, m.)* An entrance hallway within a living unit or building.

framework *(ossature, f.)* Carpentry work consisting entirely of framing or rough work.

framing *(charpenterie, f.)* The rough timber work of a house, including the flooring, roofing, partitioning, ceiling, and beams.

framing systems *(systèmes de charpenterie, m.)* See wood framing.

free floating stud *(poteau flottant, m.)* A method of assembling steel stud walls where the studs are not secured to the top track to free the backup wall from vertical loads, but still support horizontal loads. See track.

freehold See house types.

friction-fit batt *(matelas isolant à friction, m.)* Thermal insulation without vapour barrier which is held secure within the building frame by friction without additional fastening.

frieze *(frise, f.)* The middle part of the decorative design of a wall, between the architrave and the cornice. The decorated upper part of a wall, below the cornice.

frog *(clé, f.)* A hollow in the face of a brick, made during the process of manufacture to assist in bonding.

front elevation *(élévation avant, f., façade, f.)* A view of the face of a building, showing the main entrance and type of architecture.

frost heaving *(soulèvement dû au gel, m.)* The movement of soils caused by the phenomenon known as ice lensing or ice segregation. Water is drawn from the unfrozen soil to the freezing zone, where it attaches to form layers of ice, forcing soil particles apart and causing the soil surface to heave.

fruiting body *(organe de fructification, m.)* A fleshy mass of material found on decayed wood which is responsible for the production of decay fungi spores. Its presence indicates an advanced stage in the deterioration of the wood. They assume different physical characteristics depending on the decay fungi involved; some growths are bracket-like, others resemble mushrooms.

full foundation *(fondations pleine hauteur, f.)* The most common type of basement considered a living space. Many houses are built with a partial depth foundation while some older homes are built on slab-on grade that does not provide for any basement space. See also partial depth foundation.

fungus *(champignon, m.)* Micro-organism that dissolves nutrients from the materials it lives in and on, damaging these host materials.

furnace *(générateur d'air chaud, m.)* An enclosed structure in which heat is produced.

furnace, electric See heating terms, electric furnace.

furring *(fourrure, f.)* Strips applied to a wall or other surface as support for the finish material, or to give the wall an appearance of greater thickness. See also strapping.

furring channel *(profilé de fourrure, f.)* A steel member used to support interior finish; the smallest horizontal member of a suspended ceiling.

fuse See electrical terms.

fuse rejecters See electical terms.

G

gable *(pignon, m.)* The upper triangular-shaped portion of the end wall of a building.

gable end *(mur de pignon, m.)* The entire end wall of a house having a gable roof.

gable roof See roof types.

galvanized steel *(tôle galvanisée, f.)* Sheet steel that has been dipped in molten zinc to protect it against rust, used for roofing, flashing, and dampproof courses.

galvanized pipe *(tuyau d'acier galvanisé, m.)* Pipe made of galvanized steel.

gambrel roof *(toit à deux versants brisés, m.)* See roof types.

garage See outdoor spaces.

garbage disposal *(broyeur de déchets, m.)* A food waste disposer that is placed under a sink to grind food scraps put into the sink drain.

garden suite See house types.

gas-filled glazing *(fenêtre remplie de gaz, f.)* An assembly in an insulated thermal window unit that utilizes an inert gas, often argon, between panes of glass. The thermal conductivity of the gas is lower than that of air, which increases the insulation value of the window unit.

gas-fired heating See heating terms.

gauge *(épaisseur, f., calibre, m.)* A standard for measuring e.g. diameter of nails or wire and thickness of metal sheets, etc.

gazebo See outdoor spaces.

girder *(grosse poutre, f.)* A larger or principal beam used to support concentrated loads at isolated points along its length.

girths *(entremises, f.)* A band let into, or blocking fitted between structural members to keep them in proper alignment.

glass fibre *(fibre de verre, f.)* Fine strands formed by a blowing or drawing process during the melting of glass.

glass fibre insulation See glass wool insulation.

glass fibre board *(panneau de fibre de verre, m.)* High-density, semi-rigid board commonly used as a residential insulation material. Two types are available, for below grade exterior use and above grade sheathing.

glass wool insulation *(laine ou fibre de verre isolante, f.)* An insulating material composed of glass fibres which are formed into lightweight blankets of uniform thickness. Also known as glass fibre insulation.

glaze *(vitrer, glaçure, f.)* **(1)** To put panes of glass in a sash, frame, or prepared opening. **(2)** Transparent liquid applied to tiles before being fired in order to produce a glossy surface.

glazed door *(porte vitrée, f.)* A door fitted with glass panels.

glazier's points *(pointes de vitrier, f.)* Small triangular pieces of tin or zinc inserted into the rabbet or wood sash to help hold the glass.

glazier's putty *(mastic de vitrier, m.)* A mixture of whiting and linseed oil, forming a plastic substance for fixing panes of glass into a frame after installation of glazier's points.

glazing *(vitrage, m.)* A generic term for the transparent, or sometimes translucent, material in a window or door. Often, but not always, glass.

glazing bead *(baguette de vitrage, f.)* A moulding or stop around the inside of a frame to hold the glass in place.

glazing unit *(unité de vitrage, f.)* That part of a window which includes more than one glazing layer sealed around the outside edge to prevent air or moisture from entering the airspace and eliminating dirt and condensation between glazings.

grab bars *(barre d'appui, f.)* Also known as support bars. Hard plastic or metal handles installed in walls to provide support. Often used in bathrooms to help people raise or lower themselves while in a bathtub or on the toilet.

grade *(niveau du sol, m.)* The average level of the ground surface around the foundation wall. Can also mean the site surface slope or gradient, which can be modified by cut and fill.

grade line *(contour du sol, m.)* A pre-determined line indicating the proposed elevation of the ground around a building.

grade (lumber) *(catégorie, qualité, f.)* To separate lumber into different established classifications depending upon its suitability for different uses. A classification of lumber.

gradient *(gradient, m.)* The amount of a slope.

grading plan See plan.

grain *(veine, f.)* Describes the arrangement or direction of wood fibres (spiral grain, cross grain, etc.) and the relative width of the growth rings (coarse grain, fine grain, etc.).

granny flat See house types.

granular materials *(matière granulée, f.)* Materials including crushed stone, gravel or certain soils that are used for backfill or under slabs to allow for drainage of water.

grass *(gazon, m., herbe, f.)* Category of plants related to cereals which represents about ten per cent of the world's flora. A grass leaf typically consists of a sheath and a blade.

bentgrass *(agrostide, f.)* A strain of grasses normally used on golf courses.

bluegrass *(pâturin, m.)* A grass which spreads by underground stems and makes a thick sod, preferring sunny locations and well drained soils.

grass (continued)

fescue *(fétuque, f.)* A shade-tolerant grass useful for lawns which receive limited maintenance; used on poor and dry soils.

ryegrass *(raygrass, m.)* A fast-growing, rough grass; either annual or perennial, used to establish a quick grass cover where appearance is not a major factor.

grate, grating *(grille, f.)* An arrangement of steel bars that allows the movement of pedestrian traffic on top while permitting water to drain through.

gravity furnace See heating terms.

greenhouse effect *(effet de serre, m.)* Solar radiation admitted through a medium which is transformed to heat waves that cannot pass back through the medium. The process was first observed in greenhouses, where glass admitted the solar radiation, then trapped the heat . The term is now applied to the Earth's surface, where constituents of the atmosphere trap solar radiation.

green lumber *(bois de construction vert, m.)* Unseasoned lumber; lumber in which free water still remains within the cells; lumber which has a moisture content above the fibre-saturation point (approximately 25 to 30 per cent).

grilles *(grille, f.)* Bars placed over a window to entrance through the window. Also used to describe plastic inserts added to window panes to simulate old fashion checker windows. See window terminology, checker window.

ground See electrical terms.

ground cover *(plantation couvre-sol, f., tapis végétal, m.)* A mat of vegetation produced by low, spreading or creeping plants.

ground electrode See electrical terms.

ground fault circuit interrupter See electrical terms.

ground floor *(premier étage, m., rez-de-chaussée, f.)* The floor of a building closest to finish grade. Also referred to as the first floor.

grounding system See electrical terms.

grounds *(cueillies, f.)* Strips of wood or metal that are attached to walls before plastering along the floor line and around windows, doors, and other openings as a plaster stop and thickness guide.

ground water *(nappe souterraine, f.)* Free subsurface water, the top of which is the water table.

grout *(coulis, m.)* A thin mixture of cement mortar and additional water.

guard rail *(garde-corps, garde-fou, m.)* A safety barrier at the edge of an elevated platform or flight of stairs. Also called guard.

gusset *(gousset, m.)* A wood or metal plate attached to one or both sides of a joint to increase its holding power.

gutter *(chéneau, m.)* An eavestrough used to convey rainwater from the roof to the downspout.

guy wire *(hauban, m.)* A wire attached to an upright to secure it against the wind. Guy wires are often attached to stakes supporting newly planted trees, or to rooftop aerials.

gypsum board *(plaque de plâtre, f.)* Wallboard made from gypsum plaster, with a covering of paper. Also referred to as drywall.

H

H-beam *(poutre H, f.)* A structural beam, not unlike an I-beam but with wider flanges.

HERS Acronym for Home Energy Rating System. *(pas d'équivalent en français)* A method used by many U.S. states to inform consumers as to the energy efficiency of a home.

HRV Acronym for Heat Recovery Ventilator. *(VRC Ventilateur récupérateur de chaleur)* A ventilation system that provides fresh outdoor air to the house while extracting heat from the stale outgoing air. HRVs help keep indoor humidity levels under control, improve indoor air quality, and may keep heating costs down.

HVAC *(CVC Chauffage, ventilation et climatisation)* A general term which means Heating, Ventilation and Air Conditioning. It is used to describe systems in the house which are used for space conditioning.

habitable room or space *(pièce habitable, f.)* A room or space intended primarily for human occupancy.

half-bath See house rooms.

handshake *(message de colloque, m.)* In computer systems including home automation systems, an exchange of signals that acknowledges a communications link between two devices. A handshake usually not only acknowledges that a connection has been made, but that the protocols used by both devices are compatible.

handrail *(main courante, f.)* A rail used for support at the top or side of a guard or balustrade.

hard-pan *(carapace calcaire, f.)* A firm, unyielding, compact soil.

hardwoods *(bois durs, m.)* The botanical group of trees that, with a few exceptions, comprises all the broad-leaved, deciduous species. The term has no reference to the actual hardness of the wood.

harmonics *(harmonique, f.)* In building electrical supplies, the science surrounding the principal that current flows in multiples of the base current of 60 Hz on a sine wave, i.e., second harmonic is 120 Hz, third is 180m Hz. Harmonics has become an important issue in energy supply because of the increase of variable speed drives, computers, medical equipment and fluorescent lighting in the home, all of which depend on a consistent current.

hasp *(moraillon, m.)* A fastening device in which a slotted plate fits over a staple and is secured to it by means of a padlock or peg.

hatch *(trappe, f.)* A covered opening which provides access to an attic, roof, or crawl space.

header courses *(assises de boutisses, f.)* Courses of a wall in which the masonry units are all headers.

header (framing) *(élément de bordure, m.)* A wood member at right angles to a series of joists or rafters at which the joists or rafters terminate. *(enchevêtrure, f.)* When used at openings in the floor or roof system the header supports the joist or rafters and acts as a beam.

header (masonry) *(boutisse, f.)* Masonry units laid with their ends exposed on the face of a wall.

healthy housing *(maison saine, f.)* A term coined by Canada Mortgage and Housing Corporation to describe housing that is resource efficient, energy efficient, affordable, environmentally responsible and built to maximize occupant health.

hearth *(âtre, m.)* The floor and area immediately in front of a fireplace.

heat detector *(détecteur thermique, m.)* Temperature-sensitive device programmed to be activated when the temperature rises above a preset point. Often used for fire prevention and control, it can trigger an alarm or release a shower of water.

heat detector, rate of rise *(détecteur thermovélocimétrique, m.)* A mechanical device which sets off a warning bell when a sudden rise in temperature takes place.

heat exchanger *(échangeur de chaleur, m.)* A device which transfers heat from a warm to a cooler medium, normally by conduction.

heat pump *(thermopompe, f., pompe à chaleur, m.)* A heating system, usually warm air, which uses outside air, ground or water as the heat source.

heat recovery *(récupération de chaleur, f.)* The process of extracting heat (usually from air or water) that would otherwise be wasted. Heat recovery in housing usually refers to the extraction of heat from exhausted air. See HRV.

heat siphon trap See plumbing terms.

heating terms *(chauffage, m. (terminologie))*

    air conditioning *(conditionnement de l'air, m.)* The process of bringing air to a required state of temperature and humidity, and removing dust, pollen, and other foreign matter. Generally refers to systems used to cool a building.

    air requirements *(quantité d'air nécessaire, f.)* The air required by the heating system, for both combustion and dilution.

    air shutters *(registre de réglage, m.)* The vanes controlling the amount of combustion air supplied to a gas furnace.

    aquastat *(aquastat, m.)* A thermostat that senses water temperature in a boiler and controls either the circulating pump or the burner.

    Bacharach smoke number *(indice de fumée, m.)* A measure of the quantity of smoke in flue gas, taken on a paper filter with a bicycle pump-like apparatus.

    baseboard heater *(radiateur-plinthe, m.)* A radiator shaped like a baseboard having openings at top and bottom through which air circulates.

    burner, atmospheric See atmospheric burner.

    central heating *(chauffage central, m.)* A heating system in which a number of rooms or spaces are heated from a central source.

    ceramic fibre liner *(chemisage en fibres de céramique, m.)* A prefabricated flexible liner for furnace combustion chambers, required when using a retention head oil burner.

    cleanout *(regard de nettoyage, m.)* An opening in the chimney below the entrance of the flue pipe to enable residue to be cleaned out.

    clearance *(dégagement, m.)* The distance between a hot surface and a combustible material.

    coefficient of performance *(coefficient de performance, m.)* A measure of the efficiency of a heat pump.

heating terms (continued)

condensing furnace *(appareil à retour d'eau condensée, m.)* A furnace with an additional heat exchanger to condense some of the water vapour and regain latent heat.

convector *(convecteur, m.)* A heating device in which the air enters through an opening near the floor, is heated as it passes through the heating element and enters the room through an upper opening.

delayed action solenoid valve *(soupape solénoïdale à action retardée, f.)* A valve mounted on an oil burner to release oil after the combustion blower starts.

dilution air *(aire de dilution, m.)* Air required by the furnace, downstream of the final heat exchanger, to isolate the unit from outside pressure fluctuations.

downsize *(compression thermique, f.)* Reducing the firing rate and hence the heat output of a furnace.

draft hood *(coupe-tirage, m.)* The constantly open air dilution device of a gas furnace.

duct *(conduit, m.)* In a warm air system, a large pipe through which heated air is circulated throughout a house.

ductless furnace *(générateur d'air chaud sans conduit, m.)* A central furnace with no warm air registers or cold air return ducts.

electric boiler *(chaudière électrique, f.)* A hot water boiler where the water is heated by electric elements.

electric furnace *(générateur d'air chaud électrique, m.)* A warm air furnace in which the air is heated by electric elements.

electric ignition *(allumage électrique, m.)* A spark plug in a gas furnace, which eliminates the need for continuously burning a pilot light.

forced warm air *(air chaud pulsé, m.)* Air circulated through ductwork within a house by means of a circulating fan located in the furnace housing.

gas-fired heating *(chauffage au gaz, m.)* A heating system where the source of heat is either natural gas or propane.

gravity furnace *(générateur d'air chaud par gravité, m.)* A heating system with ductwork but no circulating fan.

hot water heating *(chauffage à eau chaude, m.)* The circulation of hot water through a system of pipes and radiators either by gravity or a circulating pump.

hybrid system *(système hybride, m.)* A heating system that uses two sources of energy, such as wood and oil or gas and electricity.

indirect heating *(chauffage indirect, m.)* A system of heating by convection.

induced draft fan *(ventilateur de tirage forcé, m.)* A fan located downstream of the furnace proper, which forcibly exhausts combustion products and .control air intake for combustion.

kerosene heater *(chaufferette au kérosène, f.)* A space heater, often unvented, that uses kerosene as a fuel.

naturally aspirating See atmospheric burner.

Isometric view of typical heating unit.

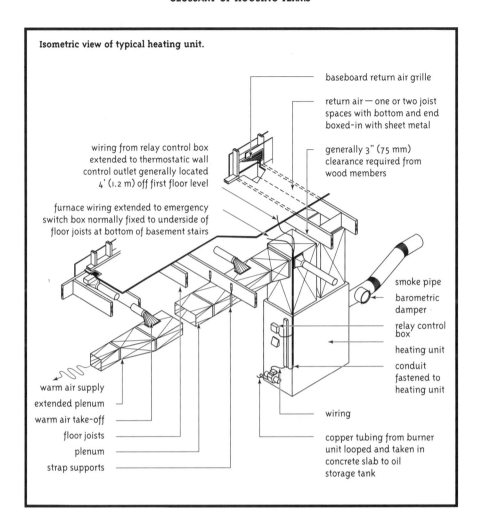

baseboard return air grille

return air — one or two joist spaces with bottom and end boxed-in with sheet metal

wiring from relay control box extended to thermostatic wall control outlet generally located 4' (1.2 m) off first floor level

generally 3" (75 mm) clearance required from wood members

furnace wiring extended to emergency switch box normally fixed to underside of floor joists at bottom of basement stairs

smoke pipe

barometric damper

relay control box

heating unit

conduit fastened to heating unit

warm air supply

extended plenum

warm air take-off

floor joists

plenum

strap supports

wiring

copper tubing from burner unit looped and taken in concrete slab to oil storage tank

heating terms (continued)

nozzle *(gicleur, m.)* The device by which fuel is sprayed and atomized into the combustion chamber, where it is mixed with air, ignited and burned.

octopus *(pas d'équivalent en français)* A gravity, warm air, ducted heating system.

panel heating *(chauffage par panneaux, m.)* Coils or ducts installed in wall, floor, or ceiling panels to provide a large surface of a low intensity supply of heat.

panel radiator *(radiateur-panneau, m.)* A heating unit placed on, or flush with, a flat surface, and intended to function essentially as a radiator.

pilot light *(bec brûleur, m.)* A small, continuously lit flame on a gas furnace or boiler which ignites the main gas flame when the thermostat calls for heat.

plenum *(plénum, m.)* A chamber forming part of an air duct system.

heating terms (continued)

plenum heater *(chauffe-plénum, m.)* An electric resistance heater, located in the warm air plenum.

radiant heating *(chauffage rayonnant, m.)* A heating system in which only the heat radiated from panels is effective in providing the heating requirements, so that only objects, not the air, are heated. This system can be installed in the ceiling, the floor or the walls.

radiation *(rayonnement, m.)* The transfer of heat from a hot surface to a cooler one across an intervening space.

radiator *(radiateur, m.)* That part of the system, exposed or concealed, from which heat is radiated to a room or other space within the building; heat transferring device.

register *(grille à registre, f.)* The outlet in a room through which warm air from the heating system flows.

retention head *(brûleur à rétention, m.)* An improved oil burner with high efficiency.

smoke number See Bacharach smoke number.

space heating *(chauffage individuel, m.)* The methods of heating individual rooms or living units by equipment located entirely within these rooms or living units, such equipment consisting of a single unit without ducts or piping.

steady state *(régime permanent, m.)* A situation of equilibrium in a heating system when the temperatures are constant . This usually takes from approximately five minutes after the furnace has come on.

steam heating *(chauffage à la vapeur, m.)* The circulation of steam through a system of pipes and radiators by any of the numerous methods employed.

transient *(régime transitoire, m.)* The unsteady condition that occurs before a heating system is in equilibrium.

transmission loss *(perte de transmission, f.)* Heat loss through the fabric of a structure.

two-pipe system *(système à deux tuyaux, m.)* A heating system in which one pipe is used for the supply of the heating medium to the heating unit and another for the return of the heating medium to the source of heat supply. The essential feature of a two-pipe system is that each heating unit receives a direct supply of the heating medium which cannot have served a preceding heating unit.

unvented space *(appareil non ventilé, m.)* A space heater where the combustion products are exhausted into the room that is being heated. There is no chimney or vent.

vent, condensing *(évent de condensation, m.)* The plastic pipe through the side wall of a house furnace to exhaust the combustion products from a condensing furnace. The system is often used in high efficiency gas furnaces which need no chimney.

vented space heater *(chaufferette ventilée, f.)* A space heater with a chimney to exhaust combustion products outside a house.

heating terms (continued)

warm air heating system *(générateur d'air chaud, m.)* A warm air heating plant consisting of a heating unit (fuel-burning furnace) enclosed in a casing, from which the heated air is distributed to various rooms of the building through ducts.

warm air heating system, forced *(générateur d'air chaud pulsé, m.)* A warm air heating system in which circulation of air is effected by a fan. Such a system includes air cleaning devices.

warm air heating system, gravity *(générateur d'air chaud par gravité, m.)* A warm air heating system in which the heat flow depends on the difference in weight between the heated air leaving the casing and the cooler air entering the bottom of the casing.

warm air heating system, perimeter *(système de chauffage périmétrique à air chaud, m.)* A warm air heating system of the combination panel and convection type. Warm air ducts embedded in the concrete slab of a basementless house, around the perimeter, receive heated air from a furnace and deliver it to the heated space through registers placed in or near the floor.

heating degree day *(degré-jour de chauffage, m.)* The number of degrees of temperature difference on any one day between a given base temperature and the mean daytime outside temperature. The base is usually 18C (64F). The total number of degree days over the heating season indicates the relative severity of the winter for a specific location.

heat pump *(thermopompe, f.)* A heating device which extracts usable heat from a medium like air or water by raising (pumping) its temperature. In its reverse mode it can be used for cooling.

heel *(pied, m.)* The end of a rafter that rests on the top plate of a wall.

height of building *(hauteur de bâtiment, f.)* The vertical distance between a horizontal plane through average grade level and a horizontal plane through: **(a)** the highest point of the roof assembly, in the case of a building with a flat roof or a deck roof, (a roof having a slope of less than 20° with the horizontal is considered a flat roof); or **(b)** the average level of that portion of a sloping roof between the highest ceiling level and the highest point of the roof.

height of building in storeys *(hauteur de bâtiment en étages, f.)* The number of storeys contained between the highest roof of a building (except for penthouses containing no dwelling units) and the floor of its first storey.

high efficiency fireplace *(foyer haute performance, m.)* A fireplace that uses advanced combustion and catalytic technologies so that it is as efficient in delivering heat as a wood stove.

high efficiency particulate arresting (HEPA) filter *(filtre absolu, m., filtre HEPA, m.)* A filter, often used on industrial vacuum cleaners, that removes many of small particulates from the air.

hip *(arête, f.)* The sloping ridge of a roof formed by two intersecting roof slopes.

hip-rafter *(arêtier, m.)* See rafter types.

hip roof *(toit en croupe, m.)* See roof types.

home automation *(domotique, f.)* The connecting of "smart" appliances, alarm systems and/or components of an HVAC system for the purpose of controlling them centrally and automatically. Home automation uses micro processor-based intelligence and communications to control the indoor environment, improve energy efficiency, and enhance homeowner convenience.

home office See house rooms.

home security system *(système de sécurité résidentiel, m.)* An alarm system used in many homes to detect undesirable events such as fire or burglary. It can be simple or sophisticated (computer controlled), but must incorporate a detector (to sense the problem) and an alerting agent such as a bell or siren (to induce the solving of the problem).

horn *(prolongement, m.)* In plumbing, the round opening on the underside of a toilet.

hose bib See bib.

hot bar See electrical terms.

hot line See electrical terms.

House as a System *(principe de l'approche systémique, m.)* A residential application of building as a system. An approach to the home that looks at the cumulative effects and interaction of the heating, cooling and other mechanical systems and the building envelope.

house rooms *(pièces de la maison, f.)*

> **basement** *(sous-sol, m.)* The part of a building that is wholly or partly below ground level. It is often finished to provide additional living space to the house.

> **bathroom** *(salle de bains, f.)* A room used for personal care, usually containing a sink and a toilet, often with a bathtub or shower.

> **bedroom** *(chambre à coucher, f.)* A room used primarily for sleeping.

> **cellar** *(cave, f.)* A basement space protected from heat that serves as a storage area for perishables. Also called cold room or fruit cellar. Also a synonym for basement.

> **closet** *(placard, m.)* A small area, usually enclosed, used for storage.

> **closet, walk-in** *(penderie, f.)* A large closet which is designed to have floor space set aside, not used for storage, to allow a person to stand within the enclosed area.

> **crawl space** *(vide sanitaire, m.)* A shallow space between the lowest floor of a house and the ground. It may be open to the outside, or be part of the heated space of the house.

> **dinette** *(coin-repas, m.)* A small space, usually attached to a kitchen, used for informal dining.

> **dining room** *(salle à manger, f.)* A room set aside for eating, usually furnished with a table and chairs.

> **family room** *(salle de famille, f.)* Large room designed as a recreation centre for members of a family.

> **foyer** *(vestibule, m., hall d'entrée, m.)* The entry area of a home. See vestibule.

house rooms (continued)

half-bath *(cabinet de toilette, m.)* A room used for personal care, consisting of a sink and a toilet.

home office *(bureau à domicile, m., cabinet de travail, m.)* A room or rooms set up as a business office within a private home. A home office usually contains office equipment such as personal computing equipment, telephone, photocopier and fax.

kitchen *(cuisine, f.)* The main room of a house in which meals are prepared.

kitchenette *(cuisinette, f.)* A small kitchen equipped with basic cooking facilities.

living room *(salle de séjour, f.)* A room used for common social activities.

vestibule *(vestibule, m.)* An entranceway hall or room that separates the main living area of a house from the outdoors acting as a buffer to cold weather. It is often used as a rest area and place to put boots and coats (sometimes called an airlock entry).

house types *(habitations, f. (types))*

cooperative *(coopérative, f.)* A dwelling unit owned by a corporation in which a purchaser acquires a share. In a co operative, rights of use and obligations of the purchaser are governed by a shareholders agreement. Also called a co op. A co operative is a form of ownership rather than a type of house.

condominium *(copropriété, f.)* A home located in a multi-unit building where the individual dwelling unit is privately owned, but the building and the land are collectively owned by all dwelling unit owners. A condominium is a form of ownership rather than a type of house.

detached house *(maison individuelle, f.)* A house containing one dwelling unit and not attached to any other building or construction. Also referred to as single detached house.

duplex *(duplex, m.)* One of two dwelling units located one above the other in a building.

freehold *(propriété absolu, propriété franche, f.)* A garden home or townhome unit where the owner owns the dwelling and lot outright.

garden suite *(pavillon-jardin, m.)* A small, usually factory-built home that is placed behind or beside the main house on a lot.

granny flat *(appartement accessoire, m.)* A colloquial term that can refer to a garden suite or to a small apartment in the main house.

leasehold *(propriété locative, f.)* A dwelling unit owned by someone not living in the unit and where the occupant has the right to use the dwelling unit on terms set out in an agreement.

link housing *(maison siamoise, f.)* A type of row housing where each home is separated by a utility room, such as a garage or laundry room, for greater privacy.

maisonette *(immeuble d'appartements en bande, m.)* A form of horizontal multiple housing in which one dwelling shares three party walls with adjacent dwellings, one wall of which may be an internal corridor. Access to the dwelling is at grade, to either the exterior or the corridor, or both.

row housing *(maison en rangée, f.)* A row of similar, attached units, often narrow and with small yards.

house types (continued)

semi-detached *(maison jumelée, f.)* One of two dwellings located next to each other in a building, separated by a common wall.

single family dwelling *(maison unifamiliale, f.)* Any housing unit provided in detached, duplex, row house, or town house unit and which is occupied by only one family.

terrace home *(maison en terrasse, f.)* One of a group of homes, the roof of which is terraced in a staircase manner and can be used at each level by the storey directly above.

town house *(maison en bande, f.)* A row of multi-level houses, each having a private outside entrance, connected by common side walls. A type of row housing unit, but with individual facades, staggered setbacks, variations in height and larger yards.

humidifier *(humidificateur, m.)* A device which may be portable or may be incorporated into the heating system's duct work and which increases the level of humidity in the house.

humidistat *(humidistat, m.)* A control mechanism which regulates the operation of a humidifier or dehumidifier, based on the amount of humidity in the house air.

humidity *(humidité, f.)* A measure of the water vapour present in the air.

humus See soil.

hybrid system See heating terms.

hydroseeding *(ensemencement hydraulique, m.)* The process of spraying a combination of fertilizer, grass seed, water, and fibrous binder onto the prepared ground in the form of a slurry; often used on steep slopes and hard-to-reach places.

hygrometer *(hygromètre, m.)* An instrument designed to measure the relative humidity of the atmosphere.

I

IAQ Acronym for Indoor Air Quality *(QAI Qualité de l'air intérieur)* A general term relating to the presence of chemical and biological contaminants in the air within a building, and their potential health effects.

I-beam *(poutre I)* A steel beam with a cross section at the top and bottom resembling the capital letter I.

ice capping See plumbing terms.

ice lensing See frost heaving.

Impact Insulation Class (IIC) *(indice d'isolement aux bruits d'impact, m.)* A rating system that rates noise transmission due to structural impact and vibration through floor/ceiling assemblies.

impedance See electrical terms.

impermeable *(imperméable, adj.)* A term applied to a soil or a material that will not permit the passage of water.

indigenous species *(indigène, adj.)* A plant or animal which occurs naturally in, or is native to a region; opposite of exotic species.

indirect siphonage See plumbing terms.

induced draft fan See heating terms.

induced draft flue system *(système de tirage forcé, m.)* A type of heating system equipped with a fan downstream of the furnace. The fan pulls gases from the furnace and propels them to the outside, thereby eliminating the requirement for make-up air.

infiltration *(infiltration, m.)* The uncontrolled admittance of air, through cracks and pores, into a building.

infrastructure See utilities.

insolation *(ensoleillement, m.)* The amount of solar radiation received on a surface.

instantaneous monitoring *(moniteur instantané, m.)* The use of sophisticated testing devices that can provide a reading within 15 minutes to an hour of the presence and quantity of a specific compound within the atmosphere of an enclosure.

insulate *(isoler, v.)* **(1)** The act of applying insulation. See insulation. **(2)** See electrical terms.

insulated spacer *(cale d'espacement, f.)* An insulated material used between glazings in an energy efficient window.

insulating wool See mineral fibre insulation.

insulation *(isolant, m.)* A material with above-average thermal resistance which inhibits the flow of heat or other forms of energy.

    blown *(isolant injecté, m.)* Low density, loose insulation material which is mechanically installed (blown).

    electrical *(isolant électrique, m.)* Non-conducting covering applied to wire or equipment to prevent short circuiting.

    friction fit batt *(matelas, m., natte isolante à friction, f.)* Batt insulation without a vapour barrier, which is held secure within framing members by friction.

    loose fill *(isolant en vrac, m.)* Insulation made from a variety of materials, with particles ranging in texture from granular to fluffy. Loose fill is excellent for filling irregular or inaccessible spaces such as roofs where the space between joists may be irregular or cluttered with obstacles. It is not appropriate for below-grade application.

    rigid *(isolant rigide, m.)* Dense insulation material that is structurally rigid, commonly available in sheets 1200 x 2400 mm. Also called board insulation.

insulation, electrical See electrical terms.

interlocking paving stones See paving.

interceptor See plumbing terms.

interstitial condensation See concealed condensation.

intrinsic heat *(chaleur intrinsèque, f.)* Heat from human bodies, electric light bulbs, cooking stoves, and other objects not intended specifically for space heating, but which contribute to the temperature inside a building.

invert *(radier, m.)* The level at the bottom of the inside of an under ground drainage pipe; often at a manhole.

irrigation *(irrgation, f., arrosage, m.)* The artificial distribution of water to promote plant growth.

island   *(îlot de cuisine, m.)* In cabinet terminology, a freestanding section of counter with cupboards or shelves underneath, usually found in a kitchen.

isocyanurate plastic foam   *(mousse d'isocyanurate, f.)* An open-celled, semi-flexible, plastic foam insulation made from a combination of isocyanurate, resins and catalysts; can also be used as an air barrier.

J

jack rafter   *(empannon, m.)* A short rafter that spans from the wallplate to a hip rafter or from a valley rafter to the roof ridge.

jack stud   *(poteau nain, m.)* A block or short stud nailed to rough door or window studding to add strength and provide a solid bearing for the lintel and nailing member for the finished door jamb or window frame.

jalousie window   See window types.

jamb   *(montant, m.)* The side member or lining of a doorway, window, or other opening.

joinery   *(ébénisterie, f.)* The fitting and joining together of pieces of wood into a finished wooden article or structure. It refers to "fine carpentry", "bench carpentry" and other fine forms of woodworking.

joint cement   *(ciment à joint, m.)* A powder which is mixed with water and applied to the joints of gypsum board.

joints   *(joints, m.)*

  broken joints   *(joints rompus, m.)* The manner of laying masonry units so as to avoid vertical joints in adjacent courses from lining up. Also the distribution of joints in lumber sheathing, flooring, lath, and panels so no two adjacent end-joints are directly in line. Also known as staggered joint or step joint.

  butt joint   *(joint d'about, m.)* Any joint made by fastening two members together without overlapping.

  construction joint   *(joint de construction, m.)* A joint between successive pours in concrete work.

  control joint   *(joint de retrait, m.)* A joint tooled or cut into the surface of concrete in order to control the location of cracks due to expansion and contraction.

  dovetailing   *(queue d'aronde, f.)* In carpentry, interlocking joints; joints made by cutting two boards or timbers to fit into each other.

  expansion joint   *(joint de dilatation, m.)* A joint in a concrete or masonry structure designed to permit expansion without damage to the structure.

  finger joint   *(joint à languettes à emboîtement, m.)* A glued joint consisting of a series of interlocking fingers, precision machined on the ends of two pieces of wood to be joined.

  flush joint   *(joint affleuré, m.)* A mortar joint of which the surface is in the same plane as the surface of the masonry wall of which it forms a part.

  lindermann joint   *(joint lindermann, m.)* A glued dovetail joint, shaped by a lindermann jointer, joining two pieces of wood edge to edge longitudinally.

Finishing of gypsum board: (**A**) nail set with crowned hammer; (**B**) cementing and taping of joint; (**C**) taping at inside corners.

A   C

sharp fold

stud

B

gypsum board

recessed edge

joint cement

tape

joint cement

feather edge

joints (continued)

matched joint *(joint embouveté, m.)* In carpentry, a joint made with tongue-and-groove material.

miter joint *(joint à onglet, m.)* A joint between two pieces of material on a line bisecting the angle of their junction.

rabbet joint *(joint feuilluré, m.)* A joint which is formed by the fitting together of two pieces of timber which have been grooved on the edge or face.

scarf joint *(joint à mi-bois, m.)* A joint where the ends of members are chamfered or shaped to correspond and are attached by bolting, gluing, etc.

tooled joint *(joint tiré, m.)* In masonry, mortar joints which are made by compressing the mortar after it has set slightly. Tooled joints present the best weathering properties.

joint sealant *(mastic de jointoiement, m.)* A setting but flexible material used to prevent the passage of liquids or gases through a joint without restricting the differential movement between the components being joined.

joist *(solive, f.)* One of a series of horizontal wood members, usually 50 mm nominal thickness, used for support in floors, ceilings or roofs.

joist bridging *(entretoise, f.)* Short diagonal braces placed between floor joists as stiffeners.

joist hanger *(étrier, m.)* A steel section shaped like a stirrup, bent so it can be fastened to a beam to provide end support for joists, headers etc.

joist restraint *(fixation des solives, f.)* A technique used to provide support and rigidity to joists and floor framing systems.

jump wire See electrical terms.

K

kerfed member *(élément rainuré, m.)* Lumber with saw cuts on the underside to permit bending.

kerosene heater See heating terms.

key plan See plan.

kiln *(four de séchage, m.)* A heater chamber for drying lumber, bricks, etc.

kiln-dried lumber See lumber.

kilowatt hour See electrical terms.

king post *(poinçon, m.)* The upright member in the centre of a simple truss, extending from the apex to the middle of the bottom chord.

kitchen See house rooms.

kitchenette See house rooms.

knee wall *(mur nain, m.)* Partitions of varying length used to support roof rafters when the span is so great that additional support is required to stiffen them.

knob-and-tube wiring See electrical terms.

knot *(nœud, m.)* That portion of a branch or limb embedded in the tree and cut through in the process of lumber manufacture. Knots are classified according to size, form, quality and occurrence.

L

lacquer See paint.

lag-screw *(tire-fond, m.)* A heavy wood screw with a square head and a coarse thread used chiefly where a bolt would not be suitable.

laminated *(lamellé, stratifié, adj.)* Layers of wood cemented, screwed, or nailed together to form a unit. The term is also applied to certain types of flooring made up of pieces of timber laid on edge instead of on their sides.

Laminated Veneer Lumber (LVL) See lumber.

landform *(forme de relief, f.)* The shape of the land surface, whether resulting from natural processes or man-made.

landing *(palier, m.)* A flat platform between a series of steps.

landing board or tread *(planche palière, marche palière, f.)* The first board on a landing immediately over the last riser.

landscaping *(aménagement paysager, m.)* The general use of plant and man-made materials on a site, as opposed to landscape architectural design which is the integration of site layout and grading in addition to the materials.

lane *(ruelle, f.)* Any passageway or right-of-way, open from ground to sky, not constituting a street, but laid down upon a registered plan and dedicated to public use.

lap siding *(planche à recouvrement, f.)* Boards used to cover the sides of buildings, the lower edge of one board being lapped over the upper edge of the board below.

latent heat *(chaleur latente, f.)* The heat required to evaporate a liquid, or the heat produced by condensing a vapour to a liquid while the temperature remains constant.

lateral thrust *(poussée latérale, f.)* That component of a load which is exerted in the horizontal direction.

lath *(latte, f.)* A building element made of wood, metal, gypsum, or fibre board fastened to the frame of a building to serve as a plaster base.

lavatory *(lavabo, m.)* A wash basin. *(toilettes, f.)* A room containing a wash basin and a toilet.

layout plan See plan.

leaching *(lessivage, m., lixiviation, f.)* **(a)** Bringing soluble substances to the surface by the passage of water through a solid such as brick or wood. In masonry, leaching often leaves a salty deposit on the surface. **(b)** The washing out of soluble nutrients and other elements from the soil by rainwater or irrigation, which alters the fertility and physical composition of the soil.

leader See plumbing terms.

lean-to *(toit en appentis, m.)* A secondary structure appended to a main building and covered with a single slope roof.

leasehold See house types.

ledger strip *(corbeau, m.)* A strip of lumber fastened along the side of a beam or stud on which joists rest.

light See window, parts of.

light standard *(lampadaire, m.)* Pole upon which an electric light fixture is mounted, normally outdoors.

lintel *(linteau, m.)* A horizontal structural member (beam) that supports the load over an opening such as a door or window. See also window, parts of.

link housing See house types.

live load *(surcharge, f.)* The aggregate weight of the movable articles in a building or dwelling, such as furniture, appliances, built-in equipment, to which a structure is subjected. The live load also includes the weight of people or occupants.

living room See house rooms.

load (dead) *(charge permanente, f.)* The weight of all construction elements in a building.

load miser See electrical terms.

loam *(terre franche, f.)* A rich soil composed of clay and sand containing a proportion of vegetable matter. See also soil.

lobby *(foyer d'entrée, m.)* A public or common entrance space in a multi-unit building.

lock nut *(écrou auto-bloquant, m.)* A nut screwed down tightly on another nut preventing the first nut from jarring loose.

lookout rafters *(chevrons en porte-à-faux, m.)* Short wood members cantilevered over, or projecting from, a wall to support an over hanging portion of a roof.

loose-fill *(isolant en vrac, m.)* Bulk insulation material used for walls in older houses and for ceiling insulation. See insulation, types of.

lot line *(limite de terrain, f.)* The line which bounds a plot of ground legally described as a lot in the title of a property. See also property line.

lot levy *(redevances d'aménagement, f.)* A fee charged by a municipality prior to construction on a lot, to help cover hard municipal services.

lot types *(genres de terrains, m.)*

    corner lot *(terrain d'angle, m.)* A lot abutting upon two or more streets at their intersection.

    gore lot *(terrain enclave, m.)* A small triangular lot.

    interior or inside lot *(terrain sur rue, m.)* A lot bounded by a street on one side only.

    through lot *(terrain traversant, m.)* A lot other than a corner lot having frontage on two public highways or streets. Sometimes called a merged lot.

louver *(orifice de ventilation à lames, m.)* A slatted opening for ventilation in which the slats are so placed to exclude rain, sunlight, or vision.

low-emissivity window (Low-E) See window terminology.

low-flow showerhead *(pomme de douche à faible débit, f.)* A showerhead equipped with an aerator, designed to reduce the amount of water used during a shower.

low-flush toilet *(toilette à faible débit, f.)* A toilet equipped with a device designed to reduce the amount of water consumed when the toilet is flushed.

low melting point fuse See electrical terms.

lumber *(bois de construction, m.)* Timber sawn, split, or hewn for use.

    air dried *(bois séché à l'air, m.)* Lumber that has been seasoned under natural atmospheric conditions.

    board *(planche, f.)* Sawn lumber less than 50 mm thick and wider than 100 mm.

    dressed size *(dimensions corroyées, f.)* The dimensions of lumber after planing to a smooth surface.

    kiln dried *(bois de construction séché au four, m.)* Lumber that has been dried in an oven, reducing shrinking and warping.

    laminated veneer *(placage stratifié, m.)* Lumber made of several thin veneers of wood glued together using an exterior grade glue. The laminating process produces a consistent, defect-free product.

    matched lumber *(bois embouveté, m.)* Lumber that is edge dressed and shaped to make a close tongue-and-groove joint at the edges or ends when laid edge-to-edge or end-to-end.

lumber (continued)

nominal size *(dimensions nominales, f.)* The ordinary commercial size by which timber or lumber is known and sold on the market, but which may differ from the actual size. For example, two by fours have nominal dimensions of 2 inches deep and 4 inches wide, but are actually about 1-3/4 inches deep and 3-1/2 inches wide.

parallel strand *(panneau de copeaux parallèles, m.)* Large beams of wood made using short, thin veneer strands that are permanently bonded through an adhesive/pressure process.

plank *(madrier, m.)* A broad board, usually more than 50 mm thick.

rough lumber *(bois de construction brut, m.)* Undressed lumber as it comes from the saw.

shiplapped lumber *(planche à feuillure, f.)* A form of matching lumber. A section one-half the thickness of the board is cut from the upper side of one edge, and a similar section from the lower side of the opposite edge.

M

machine bolt *(boulon mécanique, m.)* A bolt with a square or hexagonal head and the upper portion of the shank is not threaded.

mail and milk chute *(descente de courrier, f.)* Common in older buildings, a space within the wall used for delivery of mail and milk.

main sewer See plumbing terms.

main shut off valve See plumbing terms.

main stack See plumbing terms.

main switch See electrical terms.

main vent See plumbing terms.

maintenance *(entretien, m.)* The process of sustaining the level of physical quality of an existing building and site. Usually involves a program of inspection, cleaning, and repair activities.

maisonette See house types.

make-up air *(air d'appoint, m.)* The air required by some combustion heating systems in order to isolate the furnace from outside pressure fluctuations and to maintain a constant chimney draft. Also referred to as dilution air.

manifold *(rampe à gaz, f.)* A device for receiving flue gases from more than one flue-pipe and for discharging these gases through a single breech.

manufactured home *(maison usinée, f.)* A dwelling unit, the components of which have been built in a factory.

manufactured wood products *(produits du bois usinés, m.)* A general term referring to various types of building materials factory made from wood chips, veneers, etc.

mansard roof See roof types.

mantel *(manteau de cheminée, m.)* The work over a fireplace in front of a chimney; especially a shelf, usually ornamented, above the fireplace.

masonite *(Masonite)* High-density fibreboard made from ground wood that is pressed together under high temperatures. It is commonly used for interior panelling with veneer surface or finished exterior siding .

masonry *(maçonnerie, f.)* The use of stone, brick, or other earthen products for the erection of buildings.

masonry heater *(chauffe-maçonnerie, m.)* A wood burning device which takes advantage of tonnes of mass in the form of bricks or stone in order to store and later release the heat it produces. Stored heat can radiate for hours after the fire has extinguished.

masonry types *(maçonnerie, m. (types))*

    cavity wall *(mur creux, m.)* A wall consisting of an exterior thickness of masonry separated from an inner thickness of masonry by an air space. The materials used in the inner and outer thicknesses may be similar or dissimilar. Also called hollow wall.

    compound wall *(mur de protection, m.)* A wall made up of dissimilar materials, such as brick as a cladding over a back-up of rubble; the two materials are bonded together without enclosed space.

    hollow masonry unit *(élément de maçonnerie creux, m.)* A structural masonry unit, the net bearing area of which is reduced by voids made by mechanical means and is less than 75 per cent solid.

    hollow wall See masonry types, cavity wall.

    masonry veneer *(maçonnerie plaquée, f.)* A surface shell or cladding of masonry units attached to a backing.

    rubble-coursed *(moellons par assises, m.)* Masonry composed of roughly shaped stones laid approximately level and well bonded.

    solid masonry *(maçonnerie pleine, f.)* Masonry composed of units without enclosed spaces between them, well bonded to act as one structural unit.

solid masonry unit *(élément de maçonnerie plein, m.)* Any structural masonry unit other than a hollow unit and with more than 75 per cent solid.

mastic *(mastic, m.)* Any of various pasty materials used as a protective coating.

matched joint See joints.

means of egress *(moyen d'évacuation, m.)* A doorway, hallway corridor, exterior passageway or balcony, lobby stair ramp or other facility or combination thereof, provided for the escape of persons from a building, floor area, contained open space, or room to a public thoroughfare or other open space. Means of egress include exits and access to exits.

mechanical air filtration *(filtration d'air mécanique, f.)* The forcing of air by mechanical means through a filter screen and mechanical filtering medium. Mechanical air filtration is designed to capture particles such as dust, dander and pollen. Finer filters with denser fibres can be used to target microorganisms.

mechanical equipment *(équipement mécanique, m.)* In architectural and engineering practice: all equipment included under the general heading of plumbing, heating, air conditioning, gas fitting, and electrical work.

mechanical systems *(installation mécanique, f.)* All the mechanical components of a building, i.e., plumbing, heating, ventilation, air conditioning and heat recovery.

mechanical ventilation *(ventilation mécanique, f.)* Control of a house's ventilation through the use of a mechanical system. See ventilation.

median strip *(terre-plein, m.)* The planted or paved area which lies between two traffic lanes in the middle of a road. Also called divider strip *(terre-plein. m.)*. See also boulevard strip.

medullary rays *(rayons médullaires, m.)* Wood tissues which usually run continuously from the pitch to the bark, particularly prominent in quarter-cut oak.

meeting rail *(traverse de rencontre, f.)* The rails of a pair of sashes that meet when the sashes are closed.

membrane filters *(membrane filtrante, f.)* Used to remove more contaminants from the water supply than carbon filters, simple systems combine a carbon filter with a special membrane. Membrane filters can prevent the passage of particulate matter including radioactive particles, but do not trap bacteria.

mesh *(trellis, m.)* Expanded metal or woven wire used as a reinforcement for concrete, plaster, or stucco.

metal lath *(latte métallique, f.)* Expanded metal woven wire used to provide a base for plaster or stucco.

metal primer *(apprêt à métal, m.)* Paint, used as a protective and first coat on iron or other metals.

meter See electrical terms.

meter socket See electrical terms.

meter stop See plumbing terms.

metes and bounds *(bornes, f.)* A means of describing the location of land by defining boundaries in terms of directions and distance from one or more specific points of reference.

methane gas *(méthane, m.)* The gas produced by rotting materials such as those in landfill sites. Methane gas is flammable and can produce a hazard where construction occurs on old landfill sites.

mezzanine or mezzanine floor *(mezzanine, f.)* An intermediate floor between the floor and ceiling of any storey.

microclimate *(microclimat, m.)* The localized climate of a given area, which may differ from surrounding general climatic conditions. Microclimate is influenced by topography, drainage, vegetation, and orientation to the sun.

mildew *(mildiou, m.)* A variety of fungi that survives and grows on damp materials, including porous building materials, plants, paper, etc.

millwork *(travaux de menuiserie, m.)* Building materials made of finished wood and including such items as inside and outside doors, window and door frames, panel work, mouldings, and interior trim. It does not include flooring, ceiling, or siding.

mineral aggregate *(granulat minéral, m.)* An aggregate consisting of a mixture of broken stone, broken slag, crushed or uncrushed gravel, sand, stone, screenings, and mineral dust. See also aggregate.

mineral fibre *(fibres minérales, f.)* Fibres made from rocks (often mining waste) used as insulation material available in batts or continuous rolls.

mineral fibre insulation *(isolant de fibres minérales, m.)* Insulation made from various fibrous materials (glass fibres, mineral fibres, cotton, etc.) to produce blanket or batt insulation. Excellent to fill cavities between studs, joists, trusses, or any large and regular cavities.

mineral wool *(laine minérale, f.)* A material used for insulating buildings and produced by sending a blast of steam through molten slag or rock; common types now in use include rock wool, glass wool, and slag wool.

mitre joint See joints.

mobile home *(maison mobile, f.)* A type of manufactured house that is completely assembled in a factory, then moved to a foundation before it is occupied.

modular brick *(brique modulaire, f.)* Bricks which are designed for use in walls built in accordance with modular dimensional standards.

modular construction *(construction modulaire, f.)* Construction conforming to a pre-determined measurement unit, e.g. houses are assigned with wall lengths in units of 100 mm, thus making it possible to utilize standard-sized building materials.

modular home *(maison modulaire, f.)* A manufactured house built using modular construction.

module *(module, m.)* A standard unit of measurement in building construction.

modulus of elasticity, or coefficient of elasticity *(module d'élasticité, m.)* The ratio of the unit stress to the unit deformation. Often called Young's modulus.

modulus of rupture *(module de rupture, m.)* The value of unit fibre stress computed on the assumption of linear variation of stress when a beam is ruptured under a known transverse load.

moisture barrier *(membrane étanche à l'humidité, f.)* Any material which is used to retard the passage or flow of vapour or moisture into construction and thus prevent condensation. See also damp-proof course, vapour barrier.

moisture content *(teneur en humidité, f.)* The amount of water in a material such as in wood, generally expressed as a percentage of oven-dry weight of the material.

mold or mould *(moisissure, f.)* A fungus that grows on or in damp and decaying matter.

momentum siphonage See plumbing terms: indirect siphonage.

monolithic *(monolithe, adj.)* The term applied to a structure made of a continuous mass of material. See also construction types.

monument *(borne, f.)* A permanent marker of stone or metal set to mark a property or reference line; also used for elevation. See benchmark.

mortar *(mortier, m.)* A substance produced from prescribed proportions of cementing agents, aggregates, and water which gradually sets hard after mixing.

mortar bed *(lit de mortier, m.)* Layer of mortar on which any structural member, masonry unit, or tile is laid.

mortise *(mortaise, f.)* The cut-out in a board or unit to receive a tenon lock, hinge, etc.

moulding *(moulure, f.)* Lumber which has been worked on its side or edge to a uniform cross-section, other than rectangular to give an ornamental effect.

mound *(monticule, m., butte, f.)* A small hill usually round or oval in shape.

mountable curb See: curb, rolled.

mudsill *(lisse d'assise, f.)* Timber placed directly on the ground as a foundation for a structure.

mulch *(paillis, m.)* A layer of vegetable material, such as straw, leaves, bark, or wood chips, spread on the surface of the soil to discourage weed growth, reduce water loss due to evaporation, and protect roots.

mullion See window, parts of.

municipal stop See plumbing terms.

muntin See window, parts of.

mycelia *(mycélium, m.)* The thread-like parts of a fungus that invade a material and transport dissolved nutrients.

N

nailer (nailing strip) *(latte, f.)* A strip of material, usually wood, used to secure panels and allow for nailing of finished materials.

nailing, blind *(clouage dissimulé, m.)* A method of fastening in which the nail is driven into the edge of the board at an angle so that the head is concealed by the edge of the next board. Sometimes called secret nailing.

nail *(clou, m.)* A fastening device, usually metal, that is driven through one object into the next and is held in place by a head wider than its shaft.

nails, types of *(clou (sortes))* Based on the process of manufacture there are three kinds of nails in common use: plate or cut nails, wire nails, and clinch nails.

    aluminum nails *(clou d'aluminium, m.)* Nails made of aluminum and used for same purposes as wire nails. Also a special purpose nail for roofing, aluminum flashing, etc.

    brads *(clou à finir, m.)* Thin nails with a small head, used for small finish panel-moulding, etc.

    clinch nails *(clou à river, m.)* Nails made from open hearth or Bessemer steel wire; only used in places where it is desireable to turn over the ends of the nails to form a clinch, as in the case of battens or cleats.

    coated wire nails *(clou de broche enrobé, m.)* Nails coated with various resinous gums to increase withdrawal resistance.

    copper and brass nails *(clou de cuivre ou de laiton, m.)* Copper and cast brass nails that are used in buildings for attaching similar metal to wood.

    cut nails *(clou coupe, m.)* Nails stamped from a strip of rolled iron or steel of the same thickness as the nail and a little wider than its depth.

    wire nails *(clou de broche, m.)* Nails made from wire, of the same section-diameter as the shank of the nail, by a machine which cuts the wire in even lengths, heads and points them, and when desired, also barbs them.

natural convection *(convection naturelle, f.)* Heat transfer from one part of a fluid to another by flow of the fluid from the hotter parts to the colder without pumping.

naturally aspirating See heating terms, atmospheric burner.

neat cement *(ciment pur, m.)* A cement mortar mixture made up without addition of sand or other aggregate.

negative ion generation filter *(générateur d'ions négatifs, m.)* An air filtering system in which negatively-charged air ions impact an electric charge to the air-borne particles with which it collides. After being charged by the ions, the particles stick to the nearest surface and are removed from the atmosphere. Excellent for the trapping of visible, odorous toxic gases present in smog and tobacco smoke.

negative pressure *(pression négative, f.)* A pressure below atmospheric pressure. A negative pressure exists when the pressure inside the house envelope is less than the air pressure outside. Negative pressure will encourage infiltration and backdrafting.

neoprene *(néoprène, m.)* A firm and compressible synthetic rubber that can be used as a filler in deep joints such as those in a brick veneer.

neutral block See electrical terms.

neutral plane *(surface neutre, f.)* That plane within the house envelope which connects points on its perimeter where the interior and exterior air pressures are equal. Above the neutral plane exfiltration can occur; below it infiltration is likely to occur.

newel *(poteau d'escalier, m.)* A post to which the stair railing or balustrade is fastened.

nitrogen dioxide *(dioxyde d'azote, m.)* An air pollutant caused by high temperature combustion in the presence of nitrogen.

node zero *(sommet, m.)* In electrical and home automation applications, the point where incoming cabling and wiring comes together usually to connect to a central control system.

nominal size lumber See lumber.

nominally horizontal *(essentiellement horizontal, adj.)* In plumbing, at an angle of less than 45° to the horizontal.

non-bearing partition See partition.

noncombustible *(incombustible, adj.)* See combustible and noncombustible materials.

noncombustible construction *(construction incombustible, f.)* Type of construction in which a degree of fire safety is attained by the use of non-combustible materials for structural members and other building assemblies.

non-renewable energy source *(source d'énergie non renouvelable, f.)* A source of power derived from an expendable natural resource such as fossil fuels. See also renewable energy source.

nonslip or nonskid *(antidérapant, adj.)* A term applied to walk, road, floor, or other surfaces specially prepared to minimize slipping.

Normalized Leakage Area (NLA) *(no French equivalent)* The Equivalent Leakage Area (ELA) from a fan test divided by the area of the exterior envelope of the house.

nosing *(nez, m.)* The rounded and projecting edge of a stair tread, window, sill, etc.

nozzle See heating terms.

O

oakum *(étoupe, f.)* A treated hemp used for caulking joints.

occupant load *(charge d'occupants, f.)* The number of persons for which a building or part thereof has been designed.

octopus See heating terms.

off-gassing *(effluent gazeux, m.)* The gradual release of volatile and often toxic substances from a wide range of construction materials. These rates generally decrease over time.

offset *(ressaut, m.)* **(1)** A term used in building when referring to a sunken panel in a wall or a recess of any kind; also, a horizontal ledge on a wall formed by a change in the wall thickness at that point. **(2)** See plumbing terms.

ogee or O.G. *(talon renversé, m.)* A moulding with a profile in the form of the letter S; having the outline of a reversed curve.

ohm See electrical terms.

on centre *(entraxes, m.)* (abbr: o.c.) A term used to define the point from which measurements are taken - from the centre of one member to the centre of the adjacent member as in the spacing of studs, joists, or nails. See also centre to centre.

open stairway See stairway types.

organic solvents *(solvants organiques, m.)* A family of carbon-containing compounds used to dissolve or disperse other substances. For example, mineral spirits.

oriel window See window types.

orientation *(orientation, f.)* The direction (with respect to the points of a compass) in which the building axis lies or external walls face.

oriented strand board, or OSB *(panneau à copeaux orientés, m.)* Structural wood panel manufactured from wood strands which are oriented in the same direction and bonded together with glue. It is a high strength product made from low grade (waste) material.

outcrop *(affleurement rocheux, m.)* A surface of bare rock protruding from the surrounding soil cover.

outdoor space *(espace extérieur, m.)*

> **communal amenity area** *(aire d'agrément communautaire, f.)* An area within the boundary of a project, used by the residents on a shared basis for their enjoyment and recreation. Also called communal space.

> **outdoor living area** *(aire de séjour extérieure, f.)* An outside space immediately adjacent to, and accessible from, a dwelling, and capable of accommodating a variety of individual outdoor activities for the residents.

> **patio** *(patio, m.)* A hard-surfaced area near a dwelling, provided for outdoor activities. Normally included in outdoor living area.

> **play space** *(aire de jeux, f.)* An area furnished with play equipment or play-inducing features for children.

> **privacy zone** *(zone privée, f.)* An area adjacent to a dwelling which is restricted to exclusive use by the residents of the dwelling.

outdoor space (continued)

public space *(espace public, m.)* Publicly owned land and facilities which are open to use by the general public, such as a street right-of-way.

separation space *(espace séparatif, m.)* Open space provided around dwelling units to ensure access privacy and exposure to sun.

outdoor spaces *(espaces extérieurs, m.)*

balcony *(balcon, m.)* A projecting gallery or platform that projects from the wall of a building that is either cantilevered or supported and enclosed by a railing.

belvedere *(belvédère, m.)* A structure attached to a house (usually on its roof), designed to allow a view.

deck *(terrasse de bois, f.)* A flat-floored, roofless area adjoining a house.

driveway *(entrée de garage, f.)* A short road on private property leading from a public access street and adjacent to a building that allows parking of personal vehicles.

garage *(garage, m.)* An enclosed space designed to hold one or more automobiles. Can be a separate building or attached to a dwelling unit.

gazebo *(kiosque de jardin, m.)* A small, decorative, free-standing structure usually open on all sides.

patio *(patio, m.)* A paved or planked area adjoining a building, often used for recreation.

perron *(perron, m.)* An outdoor stairway leading up to a building entrance or a platform.

porch *(véranda, f.)* An entrance to a building often covered with its own roof.

portico *(portique, m.)* A type of porch featuring columns and a pediment.

terrace *(terrasse en terre-plein, f.)* A relatively level (paved, wooden or planted) area adjoining a building.

veranda *(véranda, f.)* A usually roofed, open gallery attached to the exterior of a building. Also known as a porch if located at the entrance.

outlet See electrical terms.

out-of-plumb *(hors d'aplomb, adj.)* A term used when referring to a member which is not vertical.

overhangs *(surplomb, m.)* Part of the home that hangs over its supporting structure, as in an overhang of the foundation. See also cantilevers.

overload device See electrical terms.

overloading See electrical terms.

P

PLC Acronym for Power Line Carrier. *(système à courants porteurs sur lignes industrielles, m.)* In home automation applications, signals which travel through a building's existing AC wiring.

P-valve See plumbing terms.

PVC Acronym for polyvinylchloride. *(PVC)* Plastic used in cold liquid pipes, siding, window frames, cable jackets, etc.

paint *(peinture, f.)* A mixture of a pigment in a liquid base that forms a thin, adherent coating when applied.

acrylic latex *(émulsion acrylique, f.)* A water-based emulsion sealant good for non-porous surfaces such as aluminum, glass and ceramic tile.

alkyd *(alkyde, f.)* An oil-based paint that has excellent covering ability and a resistant gloss finish. Commonly used on floors and in high humidity areas. It has the ability to retard moisture migration through walls and ceilings.

blistering *(cloquage, m.)* The forming of bubbles or blisters on the painted surface while the paint coat is still elastic.

chalking *(farinage, m.)* A condition in which paint deteriorates by oxidation to form a chalk-like powder.

checking *(fendillage, m.)* The act of cracking in paint.

colloidal paint *(peinture colloïdale, f.)* A paint made with pure pigments and without fillers. The pigments are not ground, but are reduced to extremely fine particles and colloidally suspended in the vehicle.

drier *(siccatif, m.)* A volatile liquid assisting the paint mixture to dry.

enamel *(émail, m.)* (1) A hard vitreous material baked on the surface of metal, porcelain, or brick. (2) A form of paint that dries with a hard, glossy surface. An enamel paint may be either of the lacquer or varnish variety.

epoxy *(époxyde, m.)* Two-part materials mixed immediately before use to constitute a paint with outstanding corrosion resistance offering a tough and stable finish.

filler *(bouche-pores, m.)* A compound consisting of a drying vehicle and an inert, pliable substance used to level out the pores or cells of coarse-grained wood such as oak.

incompatibility *(incompatibilité, f.)* Successive paint coats of radically different composition causing premature failure of the final coat.

lacquer *(laque, f.)* Various clear spirit varnishes.

latex *(latex, m.)* Low-toxicity paint made by mixing coloured pigments in a latex rubber base (natural or synthetic). It is a popular interior finish because it is water-based and washable when dry.

peeling *(écaillage, m.)* The final stage in the failure of a coat of paint due to excessive moisture in the wood behind the paint, or to incompatibility of successive coats. Some types of multi-pigment paints fail by peeling.

pigment *(pigment, m.)* The solid ingredient of paint giving it colour and contributing to the body of the paint.

plastic *(plastique, m.)* A coating applied by brush or spray, containing plastic resins.

primer *(apprêt, m.)* A base coat of paint, usually of neutral colour, which prepares a surface for a final coat.

priming coat *(couche d'impression, f.)* The first coat of paint applied to the new surface.

solvent *(solvant, m.)* A substance, usually liquid, having the power of dissolving the base material of a paint.

paint (continued)

varnish *(vernis, m.)* A transparent coating containing natural or synthetic resins which will reveal the grain and natural or stained colour of the wood it protects.

vehicle *(véhicule, m.)* The liquid ingredient which, upon drying, gives adhesion of pigment particles to each other and to the object being painted and contributes to the body of the coat.

Palladian window See window terminology.

pane See window, parts of.

panel *(panneau, m.)* (1) A large sheet of lumber, plywood, or other material. (2) A thin board with all its edges inserted in a groove of a surrounding frame of thicker material. (3) A portion of a flat surface recessed below the surrounding area, distinctly set off by moulding or some other decorative device. (4) A section of floor, wall, ceiling, or roof, usually prefabricated and of large size, handled as a single unit in the operation of assembly and erection.

panelboard See electrical terms.

panel heating See heating.

panel-point See truss terminology.

panel schedule See electrical terms.

panel radiator See heating.

panic bolt *(verrou d'urgence, m.)* A special form of door-bolt located at the middle of the door which is released by pressure. Commonly used on exit doors so that these cannot be opened from the outside but can be opened from the inside in an emergency.

parallel strand lumber, or PSL *(poutre de copeaux parallèles, f.)* Large beams of wood made using short, thin veneer strands that are permanently bonded through an adhesive/pressure process.

parapet *(parapet, m.)* A wall serving as a guard at the edge of a roof, terrace, bridge, etc.

parapet wall *(mur de parapet, m.)* That part of an exterior wall, party wall, or fire wall extending above the roof line.

parging *(crépi, m.)* A coat of plaster or cement mortar applied to masonry or concrete walls.

parquet *(parqueterie, f.)* Flooring made in geometrical designs with small pieces of wood.

partial depth foundation *(fondations mi-hauteur, f.)* A foundation that accommodates a crawl space, storage area or some other non-living space.

particleboard *(panneau de particules, m.)* Generic name for products made by gluing wood particles together to form a panel.

particulates *(particules, f.)* Solid particles (i.e., dust, smoke, pollens) that are airborne. Respirable particulates (RSP) are those particulates smaller than 10 microns in diameter which can be inhaled deeply into the lungs.

parting strip *(tasseau de séparation, m., moulure de rencontre, f.)* Also, bead. A thin strip of wood set into the head and jamb of a window frame to hold the sash apart.

partition *(cloison, f.)* The interior wall separating one part of a house from another; usually a permanent inside wall which divides a house into various rooms.

  bearing *(cloison porteuse, f.)* A partition which supports any vertical load in addition to its own weight.

  dwarf *(cloison naine, f.)* A partition of less than normal full height. A row of short studs to provide intermediate support for a long roof span.

  fire *(cloison coupe-feu, f.)* A partition designed to restrict the spread of fire between adjoining rooms or areas.

  nonbearing *(cloison non porteuse, f.)* A partition extending from floor to ceiling which supports no load other than its own weight.

party wall *(mur mitoyen, m.)* A wall jointly owned and jointly used by two parties under easement agreement or by right in law, and erected at or upon a line separating two parcels of land each of which is, or is capable of being, a separate real estate entity.

Pascal *(Pascal)* Abbreviation, Pa. A unit measurement of pressure in the SI (metric) system. House airtightness tests are typically conducted with a pressure difference of 50 Pa between the inside and outside. 50 Pa is equivalent to the pressure of a column of water of 5mm (0.2 in) at 12.9°C (55°F).

passive solar gain *(gain solaire passif, m.)* The ability of a house to receive the heat produced by the sun; sunshine entering through south-facing windows and being stored in the house's mass to be radiated afterward is the essence of passive solar gain.

passive solar design *(maison à énergie solaire passive, f.)* A house design that takes full advantage of passive solar gain by maximizing the unobstructed southern exposure in winter and placing windows on the south side.

patio See outdoor space.

paving *(pavage, revêtement du sol, m.)* A hard surfacing material on a roadway, terrace, walkway, or other area.

  asphalt paving *(pavage en asphalte, m.)* A surface material combining asphalt and mineral aggregates, usually consisting of a binding course *(couche de liaison, f.)* and the top wearing course *(couche d'usure, f.).*

  checker block paving *(pavage en damier, m.)* A surface of concrete paving blocks with open sections in which grass can be grown, in order to create an overall checkerboard pattern.

  cobble, cobblestone *(pavé rond, m.)* Small and roughly squared or egg-shaped stone.

  compacted earth *(terre battue, f.)* An area of bare soil, made dense by artificial means or by pedestrian and vehicular traffic.

  concrete paving *(pavage en béton, m.)* Surface of cast-in-place Portland cement concrete, normally installed on a base of crushed stone or gravel.

  granite setts *(pavage en blocs de granit, m.)* A surface of granite blocks of rectangular shape and of approximately brick-size dimensions.

  interlocking paving stones *(pavés auto-bloquant, m.)* Precast concrete, asphalt or rubber pavers of about brick-size dimensions, with shapes designed to interlock in order to provide mutual lateral support.

paving (continued)

patio block *(dalle pour patio, f.)* Precast concrete paving slabs available in a variety of shapes, sizes, and finishes. Normally larger than paving stones.

paving stone *(dalle de pavage, f., pavé, m.)* A paving material of stone or concrete with approximately brick-size dimensions and carefully controlled dimensions to permit narrow joints between blocks. Also called pavers.

slate *(ardoise, f.)* A fine-grained rock which can be split into thin sheets suitable for paving or roofing.

stonedust *(poussière de pierre, f.)* Residue from stone crushing; used for the finished surfacing of secondary walkways, and as a levelling layer immediately below paving stones.

pay-back *(période de récupération, f.)* The calculation of the period of time required for the energy and water savings to equal the initial cost of a retrofit project.

peat footings *(semelle de tourbe, f.)* Footings placed on granular fill laid on top of peat, possible when the peat is not too deep and when the home does not have heavy building features such as masonry fireplaces and chimneys.

peat moss See soil.

pebble dash *(crépissure, f.)* A term used for finishing the exterior walls of a structure by dashing pebbles against the freshly applied mortar mixture; also called rough cast.

pediment *(fronton, m.)* A low-pitched gable.

peeling See paint.

pellet stove *(poêle à granules, m.)* A stove that uses pellet fuel as an alternative to natural firewood to reduce pollutant emissions.

peninsula *(péninsule, f.)* In cabinet terminology, a counter with cupboards and shelves underneath with only one of four sides attached to a wall.

perennial *(vivace, adj., plante vivace, f.)* A herb-like plant which normally lives more than two growing seasons.

pergola *(pergola, f.)* A garden structure consisting of an overhead open framework supported by posts.

permafrost See soil.

permeable *(perméable, adj.)* Soil or material that permits the passage of water.

perron See outdoor spaces.

phenolic foam boards *(panneau de mousse phénolique, m.)* Insulation boards manufactured from phenol formaldehyde resin; suitable for areas where space is at a premium but high RSI values are required. Phenolic foam must be protected from exposure to sunlight and water.

photovoltaic *(photovoltaïque, adj.)* A device that directly converts sunlight into electricity. When light energy strikes the surface of a photovoltaic device, a direct current is created and can be stored in batteries.

pièces-sur-pièces French form of half timber framing with horizontal wood infill.

pier *(pilier, m.)* A column of masonry, usually rectangular in horizontal cross section, used to support other structural members.

pigment See paint.

pigtail *(queue de cochon, f.)* A short length of electrical wire.

pilaster   *(pilastre, m.)* A column or pier forming an integral part of a wall and partially projecting from the wall face.

pile   *(poil, m.)* Height of carpet fibres.

pile   *(pieu, m.)* A heavy timber or pillar of metal or concrete, forced into the earth or cast in place to form a foundation member.

pilot light See heating terms.

pipe   *(tuyau, m.)* A long tube designed to conduct the flow of something.

pitch   *(brai, m., poix, f.)* **(a)** Dark-coloured bituminous or resinous substances consisting of fusible, viscous to solid, distillation residue of tars; especially coal tars. **(b)** See truss terminology.

pitched roof See roof types.

pitting See blowing.

plain concrete See concrete.

plan   *(plan, m.)* A graphic representation of a site or building to a given scale.

> **block plan** *(plan en bloc, m.)* A plan of a building site showing the outlines of existing and proposed buildings.

> **grading plan** *(plan de nivellement, m.)* A working drawing showing the existing and proposed vertical dimensions of a site layout, by means of contour lines and spot elevations at high and low points.

> **key plan** *(plan clé, m.)* A small-scale plan which relates each part of the site to the whole; normally used in conjunction with a set of working drawings.

> **layout plan** *(plan d'implantation, m.)* A plan which shows the exact locations and horizontal dimensions of proposed siteworks, buildings, roads, and site features in relation to the existing site and structures.

> **planting plan** *(plan de plantation, m.)* A plan indicating the locations, types, and numbers of plants to be installed on a site.

> **plant list, plant schedule** *(liste des plantes, f.)* A chart used with the planting plan to summarize the plant quantities, their botanic names, size or caliper, and the manner of root preparation.

> **plot plan** *(plan du terrain, m.)* A plan indicating the location of a house on a lot.

> **site development plan** *(plan d'aménagement du site, m.)* A detailed plan illustrating the proposed arrangement of a site, including site layout, grading, hard materials, and planting. Sometimes called site plan or plot plan.

plank   *(madrier, f.)* A wooden board 114 mm or more in width, intended to be loaded on its wide face.

plank framing See wood framing.

plaster   *(plâtre, m.)* A white, often gypsum-based powder which, when mixed with water, becomes a paste that can be used to coat ceilings and walls or fill cracks.

plaster board *(plaque de plâtre, f.)* A rigid board made of gypsum plaster covered on both sides with heavy paper.

plate   *(plaque, lisse, f.)* **(1)** A shoe or base member, as of a partition or other frame. **(2)** A small relatively flat member usually of metal placed on or in a wall to support girders, rafters, etc. **(3)** A non-structural protective unit, such as a push-plate, kick-plate, etc. **(4)** See wall plate.

platform framing See wood framing.

platform lifts *(plate-forme de levage, f.)* A type of open elevator used to transport a person in a wheelchair from one floor to the other. The lifts use a twin rack and pinion gear system.

play space See outdoor space.

play structure *(structure de jeux, f.)* A structure for providing different play opportunities such as climbing, crawling, sliding, and swinging .

plenum See heating terms.

plenum heater See heating terms.

plot See building site.

plot plan See plan.

plough *(engraver, v.)* To cut a groove.

plumb *(aplomb, m., mettre d'aplomb, v.)* Vertical. To make vertical.

plumbing *(plomberie, f.)* The pipes, fixtures, and other apparatus for the water supply, venting, and removal of water-borne human wastes.

plumbing terms *(termes de plomberie, m.)*

    air chamber *(réservoir d'air, m.)* A piece of piping with a closed upper end, used in distribution piping to stop water hammer.

    air gap *(coupure antirefoulement, f.)* The vertical distance between the lowest point of a water supply inlet and the flood level rim of the fixture or device into which the inlet discharges.

    appliance *(appareil de plomberie, m.)* A receptacle or equipment that receives or collects water, liquids, or sewage and discharges water, liquids, or sewage either directly or indirectly to a drainage system.

    area drain *(drain, m.)* A drain installed to collect surface water from an open area.

    arm *(tuyau de douche, m.)* A short pipe to which a shower nozzle is attached.

    backflow *(refoulement, m.)* The flow of water or other liquids, mixtures, or substances into the distributing pipes of a potable supply of water, that may make the water in the pipe non-potable; may be produced by the differential pressure existing between two systems either or both of which are at pressures greater than atmospheric.

    backflow preventer *(soupape casse-vide, f.)* A device to prevent backflow from the outlet end of the supply system. See safety valves.

    back pressure *(contre-pression, m.)* In a drainage system, a higher pressure on the sewage side of a trap than on the fixture side.

    back pressure backflow *(siphonnage, m.)* In a distribution system, the reversal of normal flow in a system due to the downstream pressure increasing above that of the supply pressure.

    back siphonage *(contre-siphonnement, m.)* The reversal of normal flow in a system caused by negative pressure in the supply piping.

    back vent *(branchement de ventilation secondaire, m.)* A pipe installed to vent a trap or waste pipe connected to the vent system at a point above the fixture served by the trap or waste pipe. Also referred to as back vented.

    back-water valve *(clapet de non-retour, m.)* A valve installed in a building drain or building sewer to prevent sewage from flowing back into the building.

plumbing terms (continued)

branch *(branchement, m.)* A soil-or-waste pipe that **(a)** is in one storey, **(b)** is connected at its upstream end to the junction of two or more soil-or-waste pipes, or to a soil-or-waste stack, and **(c)** is connected at its downstream end to another branch, a soil-or-waste stack, or a building drain.

branch vent *(branchement de ventilation, m.)* A vent pipe connecting one or more individual vent pipes to a vent stack or a stack vent.

building drain *(collecteur principal, m.)* That part of the lowest horizontal piping that conducts sewage, clear water waste, or storm water from a building to a building sewer.

building sewer *(branchement d'égout, m.)* A pipe that is connected to a building drain 900 mm outside of a wall of a building to conduct sewage, clear water waste, or storm water to a public sewer or private sewage disposal system.

building storm drain *(branchement pluvial, m.)* The horizontal piping of storm drainage piping in or adjacent to a building that receives discharge from storm drainage piping and conveys it to the building storm sewer.

building storm sewer *(égout pluvial de maison, m.)* That part of storm drainage piping outside a building that connects the building storm drain to the main storm sewer; it starts at a point 900 mm from the outer face of the wall of the building and terminates at the property line or place of disposal on the property.

building trap *(siphon de bâtiment, m.)* A device that is installed in a building drain or building sewer to prevent circulation of air between a drainage system and a public sewer.

cesspool *(bassin d'épuration, m.)* A collecting tank that permits raw sewage to be leached into the ground with no provisions for the breakdown and treatment of the sewage.

check valve *(clapet de non-retour, m.)* A one-way valve in distribution or service piping, used to prevent backflow.

circuit vent *(ventilation terminale, f.)* A vent pipe that is connected at its lower end to a branch and at its upper end to a vent stack or is terminated in open air.

cistern *(citerne, f.)* A collection tank for potable surface water.

cleanout *(regard de dégorgement, m.)* A pipe fitting that is intended to provide access to a pipe to permit pipe cleaning.

combined sewer *(égout unitaire, m.)* A sewer that is intended to conduct sewage, clear water waste, and storm water.

cross connections *(jonction fautive, f.)* An arrangement of a piping line that allows the potable water supply to be connected to a line containing a contaminant.

curb box *(bouche à clé, f.)* A shut-off valve located between the dwelling and the municipal water main.

dielectric coupling *(raccord diélectrique, m.)* A device used to separate galvanized steel and copper distribution piping to prevent corrosion caused by electrolysis.

dip *(point d'inclinaison, m.)* The low point in a trap seal.

plumbing terms (continued)

direct siphonage *(siphonnage direct, m.)* The loss of trap seal as a result of unequal pressure conditions caused by the rapid flow of water through the trap.

distribution pipe *(conduite de distribution d'eau, f.)* A pipe to convey water from a service pipe to a fixture or outlet, and includes the control valves and fitting connected in it, but not a meter, control valve, or other device owned and controlled by the supplier of the water.

drain *(avaloir de sol, m.)* A pipe used to carry off surplus water.

drainage pipe *(tuyau de drainage, m.)* Any pipe in drainage piping.

drainage piping *(réseau de canalisations d'évacuation, m.)* All the connected piping that conveys sewage to a place of disposal, including the building drain, building sewer pipe, soil stack, waste stack and waste pipe . It does not include the main sewer or piping used for sewage in a sewage plant.

drainage system *(réseau d'évacuation, m.)* An assembly of pipes, fittings, fixtures, traps, and appurtenances that is used to convey sewage, clear water waste, or storm water to a public sewer or a private sewage disposal system, but does not include subsoil drainage pipes.

drip leg See relief pipe.

dry well *(puits d'égouttement, m.)* A covered pit with open-jointed linings through which drainage from roofs, basement floors, or area-ways may seep or leach into tile surrounding soil.

dual venting *(ventilation commune, f.)* An arrangement whereby two fixtures using a common drain are vented with a single vent attached near their junction.

faucet *(robinet, m.)* A fixture attached to the end of a pipe used for drawing off a liquid. Also called a tap.

fixture *(appareil sanitaire, m.)* A receptacle, appliance, apparatus, or device in a plumbing system that may discharge sewage or clear water waste, and includes a floor drain.

fixture trap *(siphon d'appareil, m.)* A trap which is an integral part of, or serves, a fixture and includes an interceptor serving as a trap for a fixture.

floor drain *(avaloir de sol, m.)* A drain to receive water from the floor of a building.

foundation drain *(drain de fondation, m.)* A drain installed below the level of the basement or crawl space floor to collect and convey water from the foundation of a building.

heat siphon trap *(coude anti-convection, m.)* An S-shaped loop in the hot water line leaving the hot water tank to prevent convection siphoning of hot water into the distribution piping while the tank is sitting idle.

ice capping *(amoncellement de glace, m.)* The formation of ice on top of a vent.

indirect siphonage *(siphonnage indirect, m.)* Creation of vacuum pressure on a trap seal by the rapid passage of water from another fixture through the waste stack.

interceptor *(intercepteur, m.)* A receptacle that is installed to prevent oil, grease, sand, or other materials from passing into a drainage system.

plumbing terms (continued)

leader *(descente pluviale, f.)* A pipe that is installed to carry storm water from a roof to a building storm drain or sewer or another place of disposal.

main sewer *(égout principal, m.)* The public sewer, including its branches.

main shut-off valve *(robinet d'arrêt principal, m.)* A valve capable of stopping the flow of all the water in the entire distribution system.

main stack *(ventilation principale, f.)* The principal soil, waste stack or vent stack in a plumbing system which connects the system to the open air.

meter stop *(robinet d'arrêt général, m.)* A main shut-off valve associated with a water meter.

momentum siphonage See indirect siphonage.

municipal stop *(robinet d'arrêt principal, m.)* A main shut-off valve located immediately adjacent to the municipal water main; not considered part of a dwelling's plumbing.

nominally horizontal *(essentiellement horizontal)* At an angle of less than 45° with the horizontal.

offset *(décalage, m.)* A combination of elbows or bends which brings one section of the pipe out of line but parallel with the other section.

P-valve Pressure relief valve. See safety valves.

plumbing system *(installation de plomberie, f.)* A drainage system, a venting system, and a water system.

pollution *(pollution, f.)* In water, presence of impuritiesor micro-organisms that may affect taste, appearance, odor and potability.

potable water *(eau potable, f.)* Water that is safe for human consumption.

relief pipe *(trop-plein, m.)* An overflow pipe for a temperature and pressure safety relief valve installed on a hot water tank; also called a drip leg.

riser *(colonne montante, f.)* A supply pipe that extends through at least one full storey to convey water.

rod *(furet de dégorgement, m.)* A long, flexible apparatus used to clean a drain pipe by mechanical means.

roughing-in *(plomberie brute, f.)* The plumbing system which is enclosed in the walls, ceilings, attics and under the basement floor.

safety valves *(soupapes de sûreté, f.)* Temperature and pressure (T and P) relief valves that protect hot water tanks from both excessive temperature and excessive pressure; also includes backflow preventers that prevent water from moving in both directions in a pipe.

sanitary unit *(appareil sanitaire, m.)* A toilet, urinal, bidet or bedpan washer.

self siphonage See direct siphonage.

septic tank *(fosse septique, f.)* A sewage settling tank intended to retain sludge for sufficient time to secure satisfactory decomposition of organic solids by bacterial action, and bleed liquids off to an absorption field.

service pipe *(branchement d'eau, m.)* The pipe that conveys water between the main shut off valve on the public water system and the control shut off valve in a supply system.

plumbing terms (continued)

sewage *(eaux usées, f.)* Liquid waste that contains animal, mineral, or vegetable matter in suspension or solution.

shut off valve *(robinet d'arrêt, m.)* A device that interrupts the flow of water through distribution piping.

sludge *(boues, f.)* Slushy matter produced by the sewage treatment process.

soil or waste pipe *(tuyau de chute ou d'évacuation, m.)* A sanitary drainage pipe that carries the discharge of a sanitary unit.

soil or waste stack *(colonne de chute ou d'évacuation, f.)* A vertical soil-or-waste pipe that passes through one or more storeys and includes any offset that is a part of the stack.

stack *(colonne, f.)* That part of drainage piping that is vertical and that runs from a building drain or sewage tank to the open air and includes offsets not exceeding 1,525 mm horizontal distance from the vertical stack.

stack vent *(colonne de ventilation primaire, f.)* A vertical vent pipe that is an extension of a soil-or-waste stack.

storm drainage pipe *(conduite d'évacuation pluviale, f.)* Any pipe in a storm drainage system.

storm drainage piping *(réseau de canalisations d'évacuation, m.)* All the connected piping that conveys storm water to a place of disposal, and includes the building storm drain, building storm sewer, rainwater leader and area drain.

storm water *(eaux pluviales, f.)* Rain water, melted snow or ice and water in the subsoil.

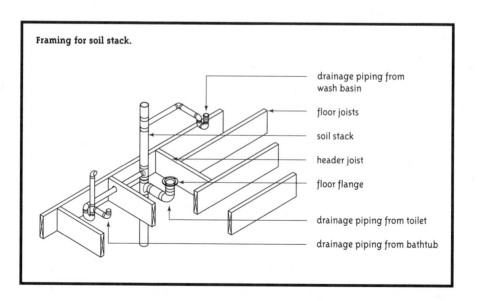

Framing for soil stack.

drainage piping from wash basin

floor joists

soil stack

header joist

floor flange

drainage piping from toilet

drainage piping from bathtub

plumbing terms (continued)

subdrain *(drain de sortie, m.)* A drain that is at a lower level than the building drain and the building sewer.

subsoil drainage pipe *(tuyau de drainage, m.)* A perforated pipe that is installed underground to intercept and convey ground water.

subsurface drain *(drain de sortie, m.)* A drain, other than a foundation drain, installed to collect water from subsoil.

sump *(puisard, m.)* A watertight tank that receives the discharge of drainage water from a subdrain or a foundation drain and from which the discharge flows or is ejected into drainage piping by pumping.

sump pump *(pompe de puisard, f.)* A pump, usually electrically operated, to remove water which collects in a sump.

T-valve Temperature relief valve. See safety valves.

trap *(siphon, m.)* A fitting or device that is designed to hold a liquid seal that will prevent the passage of gas but will not materially affect the flow of a liquid.

trap seal *(garde d'eau, f.)* The vertical depth of water between the weir and the trap dip.

trap seal loss *(perte de garde d'eau, f.)* The loss of a trap seal by water in the trap falling below the level necessary to maintain an airtight seal.

vacuum breaker *(casse-vide, m.)* A device that breaks a vacuum action and hence stops backflow.

vent stack *(colonne de ventilation primaire, f.)* A continuous run of vent pipe connected to a soil stack, waste stack or building drain and terminating in the open air.

venting system *(système de ventilation, m.)* An assembly of pipes and fittings that connects a drainage system with outside air to assure circulation of air and the protection of trap seals in the drainage system by maintaining atmospheric pressure.

water closet *(cabinets d'aisances, m., toilette, f.)* A toilet bowl and its accessories.

water hammer *(coup de bélier, m.)* A build-up of pressure in a length of horizontal or vertical pipe which occurs when a valve or faucet is closed suddenly.

water service pipe *(branchement d'eau, m.)* A pipe that is in a water system and conveys water from a public water main or a private water source to the inner side of the wall or floor through which the system enters the building.

wet vent *(ventilation interne, f.)* A waste pipe functioning also as a vent pipe.

weir *(déversoir, m.)* The high point in a trap seal.

plumb line *(fil à plomb, m.)* A strong, heavy string or cord with a weight on one end. It is used to establish a perpendicular line.

ply *(pli, m.)* Used to denote the number of thicknesses of building paper or, in plywood, the thicknesses of wood veneer; as three-ply, five-ply, etc.

plywood *(contreplaqué, m.)* A piece of wood made of two or more layers of veneer joined with glue and usually laid with the grain of adjoining plies at right angles. To secure balanced construction, it is customary for an odd number of plies to be used.

pollution See plumbing terms.

polyethylene *(polyéthylène, m.)* Very common plastic used in flexible tubing, vapour barriers, roof vents, etc.

polyisocyanurate boards *(panneau d'isocyanurate, m.)* Plastic insulation boards made out of closed cells containing refrigerant gases (fluorocarbons) instead of air used where space is at a premium and a high RSI is desirable.

polystyrene *(polystyrène, m.)* A thermoplastic material possessing good electrical insulation properties.

polysulfide sealant *(matériau d'étanchéité au polysulfure, m.)* A paintable sealant which remains flexible after curing; ideally suited for use on stone, masonry, and concrete surfaces. Ventilation is needed to remove potentially toxic vapours.

polyurethane insulation *(isolant de polyuréthane, m.)* A pale yellow insulation foam of closed cells containing refrigerant gases (fluorocarbons) that can also be used as an air barrier, but not vapour barrier.

pony wall *(mur bas, m.)* A wall consisting of short sections of wood frame sitting on top of a conventional concrete foundation.

porch   See outdoor spaces.

portico   See outdoor spaces.

Portland cement *(ciment Portland, m.)* A hydraulic cement, commonly used in the building trades, consisting of silica, lime, and alumina intimately mixed in the proper proportions, then burned in a kiln. The clinkers or vitrified product, when finely ground, form an extremely strong cement. See also cement.

positive pressure *(pression positive, f.)* A pressure above atmospheric pressure. A positive pressure exists when the pressure inside the house envelope is greater than the air pressure outside. A positive pressure difference will encourage exfiltration.

post and beam construction   See wood framing.

potable water   See plumbing terms.

power   See electrical terms.

power circuit   See electrical terms.

power venter *(ventilation à air pulsé, f.)* A device to provide mechanical draft, installed between the appliance and the vent termination. Also referred to as a sidewall vent.

prefabricated construction *(construction préfabriquée, f.)* See construction types.

preserved wood foundation *(fondations en bois traité, f.)* Also PWF. A frame wall, made of wood that has been pressure treated, that can be insulated by conventional methods.

preservative-treated *(bois imprégné, m.)* A type of construction consisting of a pressure treated wood footing plate foundation resting on a gravel drainage bed, pressure treated (PWF) bottom and top plates, studs and blocking, with pressure treated plywood as outside cladding, and a polyethylene sheet for added dampproofing. The space between the studs may be filled with insulation.

pressure control valve *(robinet pressostatique, m.)* A valve controlling a water faucet that detects the presence of an object or human body. Can be mechanical or electrical. Infrared sensors detect body presence and turn the water on or off accordingly.

pressure difference *(différence de pressions, f.)* The difference in pressure of the volume of air enclosed by the house envelope and the air surrounding the envelope.

pressure equalized rainscreen *(pare-pluie à pression équilibrée, m.)* A wall designed to prevent rain penetration by controlling the forces that drive water in a wall. Its major features are a compartmentalized cavity between the cladding and the backup wall, vents in the wall to allow moisture drainage and equalization of pressure on both sides of the cladding.

pressure treated wood *(bois traité sous pression, m.)* Wood that has been treated with chemical preservatives in order to make it resistant to deterioration caused by environmental conditions.

prevailing wind *(vent dominant, m.)* The direction from which the wind blows most often during a specific season of the year.

priming See paint.

privacy zone See outdoor space.

private *(privé, adj.)* When used with respect to a room or other space within a building, means that such room or space is intended solely for the use of an individual tenant or family.

profile *(profil, m.)* An outline drawing of a section especially a vertical section through a structural part; a contour drawing.

property line *(limite de propriété, f.)* A line, established by survey, which sets the legal boundaries of a property; may include several lots. See also lot line.

protocol *(protocole, m.)* A standard of communication used in home automation systems as in the CEBus protocol. To function properly, the devices in a home automation system must all use the same protocol.

pruning *(élagage, émondage, m., taille, f.)* The selective removal of twigs and branches from woody plants, shrubs, or trees.

public *(public, adj.)* When used with respect to a room or other space within a building, means that such room or space is intended to be used in common by the occupants of the building, their guests, or trades people.

public space See outdoor space.

puddle *(tasser, v.)* To compact clay by wetting, so as to render it firm and solid.

purlin See truss terminology.

putty (carpentry) *(mastic, m.)* A plastic substance used by glaziers, painters and finish carpenters for sealing glass in sash and filling small holes in wood such as those left by nails.

pyramid roof See roof types.

pyrolytic See window terminology.

Q

quarry tile See tile.

quarter round *(quart de rond, m.)* A plain moulding showing a quarter circle in section.

quarter sawn *(débit sur maille, m.)* Lumber that is sawn along the radius of the annual rings or at an angle less than 45° to the radius.

queen-post truss *(ferme à deux poinçons, f.)* A truss, framed with two vertical tie-posts, as distinguished from the king-post, which has but one. The upright ties are called queen-posts.

quicklime *(chaux anhydre, f., chaux vive, f.)* Calcium oxide. A white solid made by heating limestone (calcium carbonate) in lime-kilns. Used in cements and mortars.

R

R-2000 A standard owned by Natural Resources Canada, a federal government department, available to home builders in Canada and around the world. R-2000 uses the latest techniques and products to make a home extra energy efficient creating additional comfort and long-term energy bill savings.

RSI Acronym for Resistance System International. *(pas d'équivalent en français)* Thermal resistance value provided in metric terms. This is a measurement of the ability of a material to resist heat transfer and is often used to rate insulation materials.

R value *(valeur R, f.)* The overall coefficient of thermal resistance of a building material or assembly. An imperial measurement equivalent for RSI values (See RSI).

rabbet *(feuilluré, f.)* (1) A groove cut in the surface along the edge of a board plank or other timber. (2) The recess in a brick jamb which receives a window frame. (3) The recess in a door frame to receive the door.

rabbet joint See joints.

racked joint *(joint rectangulaire creux, m.)* Joints in masonry veneer where the mortar is grooved out to behind the face of the wall.

radiant heating See heating terms.

radiant stove *(poêle à rayonnement, m.)* A wood stove that supplies heat to a room by direct radiation compared to other wood stoves that use convective air flow. Cast iron stoves and those with heavy steel plate surfaces are usually of the radiant type.

radiation See heating terms.

radiator See heating terms.

radio outlet See electrical terms.

radius of curvature *(rayon de courbure, m.)* The distance between the centre line of a circular section of road, walkway, or curb and the centre of the corresponding circle.

radon gas *(radon, m.)* An odorless and colourless, naturally occurring radioactive gas formed by the disintegration of radium, which is found in most soils; it can enter a house from the soil beneath and around the house foundation, or through the floor drain. Carcinogenic with prolonged exposure.

raft foundation *(radier, m.)* A layer of concrete, usually reinforced, extending under the whole area of a building and projecting outside the line of its walls; normally used to provide a foundation in cases where the ground is unduly soft or the load to be carried is unduly heavy.

rafter See truss terminology.

(A) ceiling and roof framing with ridge board: *(1)* each rafter toenailed to ridge board with four 2 1/4 in. (57 mm) nails or end-nailed with three 3 1/4 in. (82 mm) nails; *(2)* 1 x 4 in. (19 x 89 mm) strip nailed to top of collar braces at their centre with two 2 1/4 in. (57 mm) nails when the braces are more than 8 ft. (2.4 m) long; *(3)* ceiling joists butted with splice plate over centre bearing partition. Joists also nailed to each part of rafters; *(4)* collar brace used as intermediate support for rafters nailed to each pair of rafters with three 3 in. (76 mm) nails at each end; *(5)* ceiling joists toenailed to top wall plate with two 3 1/4 in. (82 mm) nails, one each side; *(6)* rafter.

(B) jack rafter nailed to hip rafter with two 3 1/4 in. (82 mm) nails.

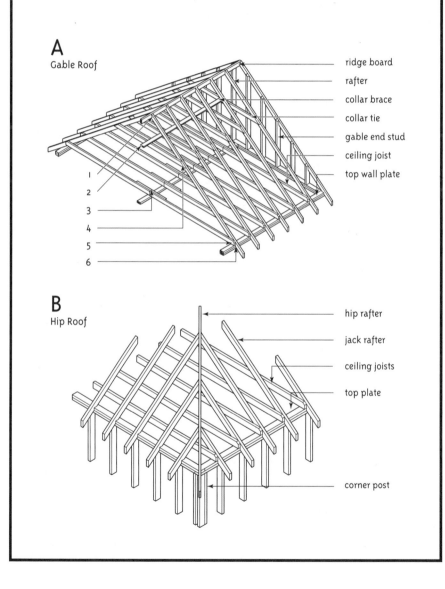

A

Gable Roof

ridge board
rafter
collar brace
collar tie
gable end stud
ceiling joist
top wall plate

1
2
3
4
5
6

B

Hip Roof

hip rafter
jack rafter
ceiling joists
top plate
corner post

rafter types *(chevron, m. (types))*

    hip rafter *(arêtier, m.)* The rafter which forms the hip of a roof.

    jack rafter *(empannon, m.)* A short rafter that spans from the wall plate to a hip rafter or from a valley rafter to the roof ridge.

    lookout rafter *(chevrons en porte-à-faux, m.)* Short wood members cantilevered over, or projecting from, a wall to support an over hanging portion of a roof.

    valley rafter *(chevron de noue, m.)* The rafters which are located at the centre of roof valleys to support the jack rafters.

rail *(traverse, f.)* A piece of timber or metal extending from one post to another, as in fences, balustrades, staircases, etc. In framing and panelling the horizontal pieces are called rails, and the perpendicular stiles.

rail post *(poteau de rampe, m.)* A newel post.

railroad tie *(traverse de chemin de fer, m.)* A large piece of lumber, generally 150 x 200 mm in cross-section; originally designed to support the rails of a railroad track but commonly used for general site construction.

rain penetration *(pénétration de l'eau de pluie, f.)* The term used to describe rain water which penetrates siding or other exterior veneer when openings are available and when there are sufficient forces to move the water inward.

rainscreen *(pare-pluie, m.)* A wall designed to prevent rain penetration by providing a cavity between the cladding and the backup wall and vents in the wall to allow moisture drainage. See pressure equalized rainscreen.

rain water leader (r.w.l.) *(descente pluviale, f.)* A downpipe from a roof or gutter, located inside a building and designed to carry water from roofs to a drain or to the ground surface.

rake *(inclinaison, f.)* An incline, as in a pitched roof. The end of a wall that slopes or rakes back; slope.

ramp *(pente, rampe, f.)* A sloping surface which provides a pedestrian or vehicular connection between two levels.

random bond *(maçonnerie en moellons bruts, f.)* A type of masonry which the masonry units are not laid in any regular pattern, but are laid as a hit-and-miss bond.

range (stove) *(cuisinière, f.)* A kitchen appliance having heating elements on a flat surface, usually combined as a unit with an oven.

range hood *(hotte, f.)* A formed canopy over a range that usually contains an electric light and exhaust fan vented to the outside designed to evacuate smoke and fumes produced from cooking.

receptacle (electric) *(boîtier, m.)* A contact device installed in an outlet for the connection of a portable lamp or appliance by means of a plug and flexible cord.

recess *(retrait, m.)* An indentation in the line of a wall as an alcove.

recycled materials *(matériaux recyclés, m.)* Materials that are reused after some processing. For example, many construction products on the market today use recycled content.

register See heating terms.

rehabilitation *(réhabilitation, remise en état, f.)* Improvement of a building or site to return it to an acceptable condition.

reinforced concrete construction See construction types.

reinforcement, ratio of *(rapport d'armature, m.)* **(1)** The ratio of the effective area of the reinforcement cut by a section of a beam or slab to the effective area of the concrete at that section. **(2)** The ratio of the area of longitudinal bars in a column to the total area within a protective envelope. **(3)** The ratio of the volume of the spiral reinforcement to the total volume within the outer circumference of the spirals of a spirally reinforced column.

reinforcing bar *(barre d'armature, f.)* A steel rod embedded in concrete in order to provide resistance to tension stresses.

reinforcing mesh *(treillis métallique ou d'armature, m.)* A grid of welded steel wires used to resist tension stresses in concrete slabs. Also called welded wire mesh.

reinforcing steel *(acier d'armature, m.)* Steel bars used in concrete construction for giving added strength; such bars are of various sizes and shapes.

relative humidity *(humidité relative, f.)* The percentage of the existing partial pressure of the water vapour in a space to the saturation pressure at the same temperature; for example, air containing one half the amount of moisture it is capable of holding has a relative humidity of 50 percent.

relief pipe See plumbing terms.

rendering *(crépi, m.)* The surface treatment of a concrete or masonry wall to improve its appearance or increase its resistance to water penetration.

renewable energy source *(source d'énergie renouvelable, f.)* Sources of energy such as wind power and solar heat that are inexhaustible or derived from organic matter which reproduces itself continually, such as wood or moss. See nonrenewable energy source.

renovation *(rénovation, f.)* The act of restoring, changing or improving a structure or room.

restoration *(restauration, f.)* The process of returning a building or site to its original appearance.

retaining wall *(mur de soutènement, m.)* **(1)** Any wall erected to hold back or support a bank of earth. **(2)** Any wall subjected to lateral pressure other than wind pressure . **(3)** An enclosing wall built to resist the lateral pressure of internal loads.

retention head See heating terms.

retention pond See site drainage.

retrofitting *(amélioration thermique, f.)* Upgrading an existing structure or system to increase performance. Often used specifically in relation to energy retrofitting which is the upgrading of a house to improve its energy efficiency. This includes adding insulation, caulking, weather stripping, replacing windows and doors and improving the heating system.

return air duct *(conduit de reprise, m.)* An opening allowing cool air to be returned to the heating chamber of a forced air furnace. Also called, cold air return.

re-used materials *(matériaux réutilisés, m.)* Materials that are re-used without any re-manufacturing or processing. Materials that lend themselves to re-use are flooring, sinks, staircases, doors, etc.

ribband *(lambourde, f.)* A piece of lumber notched into or nailed onto the back of studs to support floor joists or ceiling joists in balloon frame construction. Also known as a ribbon.

ribbon See ribband.

ridge *(faîte, m.)* The summit line of a roof; the line on which the rafters meet.

ridge beam *(poutre faîtière, f.)* A horizontal structural member usually 50 mm thick, supporting the upper ends of rafters.

ridge board *(planche faîtière, f.)* A horizontal member, usually 18 mm thick, at the upper end of the rafters, to which these rafters are nailed.

ridge roof See roof types.

ridge vent *(évent de faîte, m.)* A special sheet metal or plastic vent which is along the ridge of the roof.

rift sewn See quarter sawn.

right-of-way *(emprise, f.)* The strip of public property within which a road or other public facility may be constructed.

rigid materials *(matériaux rigides, m.)* Refers to materials that have enough rigidity to be free standing and fastened with nails or screws, such as rigid insulation.

rings, annual growth *(anneaux de croissance annuelle, m.)* The growth layer put on a tree in a single growth year and comprising spring wood and summer wood.

ripping *(refente, f.)* The sawing of wood parallel to the grain.

rip-rap *(enrochement, m.)* Stones or other material placed on a slope to prevent erosion, or to support the embankment.

rise See truss terminology. See also riser.

riser *(contremarche, f.)* (1) The vertical board under the tread in stairs. (2) In plumbing, a supply pipe that extends through at least one full storey to convey water.

rocker switch *(commutateur à berceau, m.)* A large switch that can be turned on or off by a light touch.

rod See plumbing terms.

roman bathtub See bathtub, roman.

roof joist See joists.

roof space See attic.

roof tile See tile.

roof types *(toit, m. (types))*

    curb *(toit brisé, m.)* A roof in which the slope is broken on two or more sides; so called because a horizontal curb is built at the plane where the slope changes.

    deck See Mansard.

    flat *(toit plat, m.)* A roof which is flat or one which is pitched just enough to provide drainage.

    flat-pitch *(toit à pente douce, m.)* A roof with only a moderately sloping surface.

    gable *(toit à pignon, m.)* A ridge roof which terminates in a gable.

    gambrel *(toit à deux versants brisés, m.)* A type of roof which has its slope broken by an obtuse angle, so that the lower slope is steeper than the upper slope.

roof types (continued)

hip *(toit en croupe, m.)* A roof which has all sides sloping up to a centre point or ridge, ie. a roof which has four sloping sides that meet at four hips and a ridge.

Mansard *(toit en mansarde, m.)* A type of curb roof in which the pitch of the upper portion of a sloping side is slight and that of the lower portion steep. The lower portion is usually interrupted by dormer windows.

monitors *(toit à lanterneau, m.)* A type of gable roof commonly used on industrial buildings, which has a raised portion along the ridge with openings for light and/or air.

pavilion *(toit-pavillon, m.)* A roof which forms a figure of more than four straight sides.

pent *(toit en appentis, m.)* A roof other than a lean-to roof, which has a single sloping surface.

pitched *(toit en pente, m.)* A roof which has one or more sloping surfaces pitched at angles greater than necessary for drainage.

polygonal *(toit polygonal, m.)* A roof which forms a figure bounded by more than four straight lines.

pyramid *(toit en pyramide, m.)* A hip roof which has four sloping surfaces, usually of equal pitch, that meet at a peak.

ridge *(toit à deux versants, m.)* A roof with two opposite slopes meeting at the top, and with a gable at either end.

roof deck, roof garden *(toit-terrasse, m., jardin-terrasse, m.)* An area designed for residents' communal use on the roof of a building or other structure.

shed *(toit de shed, m.)* A roof with only one set of rafters, falling from a higher to a lower wall.

room or space, habitable *(pièce, f., espace habitable, m.)* A room or space intended primarily for human occupancy.

root-bound *(profondement enraciné, adj.)* Describes a plant with roots that have become so crowded that plant growth is affected.

rot *(pourriture, f.)* The decomposition of wood or other organic material by certain types of bacteria or fungi.

rose *(rosette, f.)* The wide, flat part of a doorknob that fits snugly against the door.

rotary cut veneer *(placage à coupe rotative, m.)* Veneer cut by revolving a log against a knife running the length of the log, set in such a manner as to cut off from the log a thin sheet of a definite thickness and continuous length.

roughcast *(gobetis, m.)* A type of external plastering in which small sharp stones are mixed, and which, when wet, is forcibly thrown or cast against the surface being coated. See also stucco.

rough grading *(nivellement préliminaire, m.)* The initial modification of site levels. Usually carried out with bulldozer or other heavy equipment; applies normally to subsoil rather than topsoil.

roughing-in See plumbing terms.

rough lumber See lumber.

rough opening *(ouverture brule, f.)* An unfinished window or door opening.

row housing See house types.

rubble *(moellons bruts, m., maçonnerie brute, f.)* Masonry of rough, undressed stones. When only the roughest irregularities are knocked off, it is called scabbled rubble, and when the stones in each course are rudely dressed to nearly a uniform height, ranged rubble. See also masonry types.

run *(course, f.)* The horizontal stringer measurement used in stair framing.

running bond See stretching bond.

runoff See site drainage.

S

saddle See chimney saddle.

safety plugs *(bouchon de sécurité, m.)* Plastic plugs that insert into electrical outlets as a safety measure for children.

safety switch See electrical terms.

safety valves See plumbing terms.

sandblasting *(sablage, décapage au jet de sable, m.)* The process of scouring a surface with a powerful sand jet for cleaning or adding surface texture.

sanitary sewer *(égout sanitaire, m.)* An underground conduit for the purpose of conveying waste water and sewage from a building; as opposed to storm sewer for rain and surface water.

sanitary unit See plumbing terms.

sapwood *(aubier, m.)* The outer layers of the tree containing living cells. The sapwood is generally lighter in colour than the heartwood.

sash *(châssis, m.)* The framework which holds the glass in a window.

sash balance *(dispositif de suspension, m.)* In double-hung windows, a device, usually operated with a spring, designed to counter balance the window sash without the use of weights, pulleys, and cord.

sash frame *(encadrement de fenêtre, m.)* The outer frame with sill in which the sliding sashes or casements are suspended.

sash types *(châssis, m. (types))*

> **awning** *(châssis-auvent, m.)* A partially movable sash hinged at the top, and opening either outwards or inwards.

> **casement** See window types.

> **double-hung** See window types.

> **fixed** *(châssis fixe, m.)* A single sash fastened permanently in a frame so that it cannot be raised, lowered, or swung open.

> **hopper** *(châssis-trémie, m.)* A partially movable sash hinged at the bottom and opening inwards.

> **pivoted** *(châssis pivotant, m.)* A sash that swings open or shut by revolving on pivots at either side of the sash or at top and bottom.

sash types (continued)

single-hung *(châssis à guillotine à ouvrant simple, m.)* A window frame containing a pair of vertical sliding sashes in which only one sash is movable, usually the lower, in contrast to a double-hung sash.

sliding *(châssis coulissant, m.)* A sash which moves horizontally on a tongue or track.

scaffold, scaffolding *(échafaudage, m.)* A temporary erection of timber or steelwork, used in the construction, alteration, or demolition of a building to support workers, their tools, and materials.

scant *(faible, adj.)* Implies dimensions in sawn lumber slightly under the standard dressed dimensions.

scantling *(bois équarri, m.)* A small beam of less than 125 mm in depth and breadth.

scarf joint See joints.

scratch coat *(couche striée, f.)* The first coat of plaster or stucco which is scratched to form a bond for the second coat.

scribing *(trusquinage, m.)* Fitting woodwork to an irregular surface.

sealant *(matériau d'étanchéité, m.)* A flexible material used on the inside (or outside) of a building to seal gaps in the building envelope in order to prevent uncontrolled air infiltration and exfiltration.

sealant, acoustic *(mastic acoustique, m.)* A nonhardening sealant that does not adhere to paint but bonds to most surfaces, especially metal, concrete and gypsum board; particularly useful for sealing joints in polyethylene and vapour barriers.

sealant, acrylic latex See acrylic latex sealant.

sealer *(apprêt bouche-pores, m.)* A liquid applied directly over uncoated wood for the purpose of sealing the surface.

seasoning *(séchage, m.)* The act of drying lumber, either naturally or artificially in a kiln; the removal of moisture from wood to improve its serviceability.

security system See home security system.

segregation *(désagrégation, f.)* The separation of coarse aggregate from the mortar fraction of concrete which usually results in the formation of rock pockets or honeycombing.

selects *(de choix)* A word used in the lumber industry to imply upper grades; for certain species, particularly hardwoods, it refers to a specific grade.

self siphonage See plumbing terms, direct siphonage.

semi-detached See house types.

septic bed *(champ d'épuration, m.)* An area adjacent to a septic tank in which an underground network of perforated pipes distributes the effluent from the septic tank evenly into the soil.

septic tank See plumbing terms.

service box See electrical terms.

service head See electrical terms.

service lines See electrical terms.

service mast See electrical terms.

service pipe See plumbing terms.

serviced lot *(terrain viabilisé, m.)* A parcel of land with ready connections available to public utilities, communications (telephone and cable television) and road transportation.

servitude See easement.

setback *(recul, m.)* **(1)** The horizontal distance between the faces of the exterior wall of one storey and the exterior wall next above it, where a lower storey extends beyond a higher storey. **(2)** The horizontal distance between the wall of a building and the adjacent street line.

settlement *(affaissement, m., tassement, m.)* The sinking of an area after construction; often caused by inadequate soil compaction.

sewage See plumbing terms.

sewer, main See plumbing terms, main sewer.

sewer, storm See plumbing terms, building storm sewer.

shake *(bardeau de fente, m.)* A shingle split (not sawn) from a block of wood and used for roofing and siding.

shakes *(gerçures, f.)* Defects originating in a living tree due to frost, wind, or other causes, or occurring through injury in felling, driving, etc. which later show in the manufactured lumber, most commonly as partial or complete separation between the growth rings.

shared wall *(mur mitoyen, m.)* The same wall used for two separate housing units such as those in semi-detached and row house buildings. Also referred to as common wall. See also party wall.

shear *(cisaillement, m.)* The stress that resists the tendency of two equal parallel forces acting in opposite directions to cause two adjoining planes of a body to slide one on the other.

sheathing *(revêtement intermédiaire, m.)* Lumber (usually matched) or other material used to cover the framework of buildings on the exterior.

sheathing paper *(papier de revêtement, m.)* A semi-permeable paper treated with tar or asphalt and used under exterior wall cladding as protection against the passage of water or air.

shed roof See roof types.

shelter tubes *(galeries souterraines, f.)* Tunnels constructed by subterranean termites as a means of protection while moving between the subterranean colony and the wood being infested. Consists of a mixture of wood chewings and excrement.

shim *(cale de réglage, f.)* A thin piece of material (sometimes tapered) used to fill in space between objects.

shingle *(bardeau, m.)* A relatively thin and small unit of roofing partially laid in overlapping layers as a roof covering or as cladding on the sides of buildings.

shiplap See lumber.

shoe mould *(plinthe, f.)* For interior finish, a moulding strip placed against the baseboard at the floor; also called base shoe or carpet strip.

shoring *(étayage, m.)* The method of temporarily supporting, by props of timber or other material, buildings and the sides of excavations.

short circuit See electrical terms.

shut-off valve See plumbing terms.

shutter, thermal *(volet isolant, m.)* An adjustable part of a window assembly that can seal the opening in order to reduce heat loss.

Sick Building Syndrome Acronym, SBS *(Syndrome des édifices hermétiques, m.)* A health condition which emerged in the 1970s as a result of energy conservation practices, especially the restriction of air flow. A general term for a series of symptoms. Sufferers exhibit transient symptoms which could include any or all of: fatigue; headaches; eye, nose and throat complaints; and upper respiratory problems. Symptoms may diminish or disappear when the sufferer is removed from the building. More common in office buildings than in houses.

siding *(bardage, m.)* In wood-frame construction, the material other than masonry or stucco used as an exterior wall covering.

silicone sealant *(matériau d'étanchéité au silicone, m.)* A solvent-free silicone compound that is highly durable and excellent for large moving joints. Ventilation is required during application and curing.

sill *(seuil, m.)* The horizontal member forming the bottom of an opening such as a door or window. See also window, parts of.

sill plate *(lisse basse, f.)* A structural member anchored to the top of a foundation wall, upon which the floor joists rest.

single family dwelling See house types.

sink *(évier, m.)* A receptacle for general washing or for receiving liquid wastes.

site drainage *(drainage du site, m.)* The removal of surface water from a site by natural run-off or through a storm sewer system.

> **culvert** *(ponceau, m.)* A pipe or channel to carry water under a roadway or other obstruction.

> **ditch** *(fossé, m.)* A drainage channel generally with a V-shaped profile, deeper than it is wide.

> **farm drain** *(drain agricole, m.)* A system of draining water from the surface of fields or grass areas by the use of ditches filled with gravel; perforated pipes may also be used. Sometimes called french drain.

> **manhole** *(regard, m.)* A chamber constructed to give inspection and maintenance access to a sewer, water main, or other underground service.

> **retention pond** *(bassin de rétention, m.)* A basin in which sudden influxes of surface runoff are held temporarily before being released gradually into the drainage system.

> **runoff** *(ruissellement, m.)* Excess surface water which flows over a site instead of percolating through the soil after precipitation.

> **storm sewer** *(égout pluvial, m.)* An underground pipe that receives storm water runoff from surface inlets as opposed to a sanintary.

> **sewer** *(égout séparatif, m.)* An underground pipe that carries waste water and sewage from buildings.

> **swale** *(rigole, f.)* A small channel that is usually grassed and is wider than deep.

site furniture *(mobilier extérieur, m.)* All accessories which are provided on a site, such as benches, refuse containers, and light standards. See also street furniture.

site preload *(charge de chantier, f.)* Creating a certain depth with sand or gravel on a building site, usually to compress peat.

skylight *(lucarne faîtière, f.)* Any cover or enclosure placed above a roof opening to provide for the admission of natural light.

slab *(dalle, f.)* A thick, flat object. **(1)** A door without hardware and hinges. **(2)** The outside piece taken from a log in sawing it. **(3)** A concrete construction that is thick and flat.

slab construction *(construction à dalle, f.)* A form of construction without excavation, with a concrete slab as the floor usually supporting the superstructure.

slaking *(extinction de la chaux, f.)* The process of combining quicklime with water.

sleeper *(sous-poutre, f.)* Any horizontal timber laid on the ground to distribute a load from a post. Also a strip of wood fastened to the top of a concrete slab to support a wood floor.

slope *(pente, f.)* An inclined area on the earth's surface which is measured as a ratio between vertical drop and horizontal distance, and is often expressed in per cent. Also called gradient. See also truss terminology.

sludge See plumbing terms.

slump *(affaissement, m.)* A test which specifically measures the amount of sinking of freshly moulded concrete; used as an indication of the stiffness and eventual strength of the concrete.

smart appliance *(appareil intelligent, m.)* A home appliance that contains a microprocessor and is capable of receiving and sending signals to a control unit in a home automation system.

smart house *(maison intelligente, f.)* A dwelling containing automated systems that control such home components as security systems, zone heating and cooling, entertainment systems, etc. known generally as home automation.

smoke alarm *(détecteur de fumée, m.)* A safety device designed to issue a warning sound upon detecting the presence of smoke.

smoke chamber *(boîte à fumée, f.)* That part of a fireplace system which connects the fireplace to the chimney and allows a channelling of the flue gases to occur.

smoke control zone *(zone de contrôle de la fumée, f.)* A compartment within a floor area which is separated from the remainder of the floor area in such a way as to be smoke tight for a predicted period of time.

smoke detector *(détecteur de fumée, m.)* A device containing a sensor that triggers an alarm when in contact with smoke.

smoke pipe *(tuyau de raccordement, m.)* A pipe conveying products of combustion from a solid or liquid fuel-fired appliance to a chimney flue.

snap header, or false header *(fausse boutisse, f.)* A half length of brick sometimes used in brick facing placed end on.

sod *(gazon en plaques, m.)* A matting of grass and soil, which is cut just below the roots and then used on a new site to provide quick grass cover.

soffit *(sous-face, f.)* The underside of elements of a building, such as staircases, roof overhangs, beams, etc.

softwood *(bois tendre, m.)* The timber of trees belonging to the botanical group gymnosperms, i.e. conifers or evergreens.

soil *(sol, m.)* Earth material, derived from rock and modified by climatic and organic processes. Top soil is generally more fertile and suitable for grass and other plant growth than lower layers of soil.

coarse-grained *(sol grossier, m.)*
(a) **cobbles and boulders** *(pierres des champs, f. et gros cailloux, m.)* Cobbles are 75 - 200 mm in size and boulders are greater than 200 mm.
(b) **gravel** *(gravier, m.)* Smaller than 75 mm but larger than No. 4 sieve (approximately 5 mm).
(c) **sand** *(sable, m.)* Smaller than No. 4 sieve but larger than No. 200 sieve, particles are not visible to the naked eye.
(d) **sandy loam** *(terre sablonneuse, m.)* Soil containing 50 to 80 per cent sand particles, less than 50 per cent silt particles, and less than 20 per cent clay.
(e) **till** *(sol morainique, m.)* An unstratified glacial deposit of boulders, pebbles, boulder flour, and boulder clay.

fine-grained *(grain fin)*
clay *(argile, f.)* A very fine-grained material possessing appreciable dry strength. When moist, sticks to fingers and does not wash off readily. Not gritty to the teeth. When moist, a shiny surface is imparted when stroked with knife blade.
(a) **clay loam** *(terre argileuse, m.)* A soil containing from 20 to 50 per cent sand particles, 20 to 30 per cent clay particles, the remainder being silt particles.
(b) **clay soil** *(sol argileux, f.)* A soil containing over 65 per cent clay particles.
(c) **silt** *(limon, m.)* A loose sedimentary material. Powders easily when dry, only slight dry strength. Gritty to the teeth. Dries rapidly. No shine imparted when moist and stroked with knife blade.

organic *(organique)*
(a) **humus** *(humus, m.)* The material resulting from decomposing organic matter in the soil.
(b) **organic material** *(terre organique, f.)* Fibrous structure usually brown or black when moist. Spongy. Usually has characteristic odour. Descriptive terms: organic terrain including muskeg, peat, and sphagnum bog.
(c) **partly organic** *(terre partiellement organique, f.)* Organic clay, organic silt, etc. Depending on amount of organic material, these soils usually have some of the characteristics of their inorganic counterparts. Usually highly compressible (spongy); usually have characteristic odour.
(d) **peat moss** *(mousse de tourbe, f.)* Partially decomposed plant material, often used as a mulch and soil amendment.

other soils *(autres sols)*
acid soil *(sol acide, m.)* Typically found in a coniferous forest, a soil with a pH value below 6.6; based on a 1 to 14 rating of acid to alkaline, with 7.0 being neutral.
alkaline soil *(sol alcalin, m.)* A soil with a pH over 7.3, such as that found in many arid regions. An alkaline soil is often poorly drained.
alluvium *(alluvion, f.)* A soil consisting of material which has been deposited by running water.
permafrost *(pergélisol, m.)* A layer of soil or bedrock that is permanently frozen; found throughout northern regions and scattered at higher elevations in other regions of Canada.

soil-or-waste pipe See plumbing terms.

soil-or-waste stack See plumbing terms.

soil test *(étude des sols, f.)* A sampling of an area to determine the characteristics of its soils and to map their location; usually accomplished by borings and subsequent laboratory analysis.

solarium *(solarium, m.)* An attached greenhouse-like space for general use as living space.

solar heat gain coefficient *(coefficient de gains solaires, m.)* A term used in the passive solar heating field to describe the amount of heat gained through windows during the heating season. Net solar gain refers to the solar heat gain less the heat losses through the windows.

solar system, active *(système solaire actif, m.)* A solar system that uses mechanical devices such as fans and pumps to collect, store, and distribute the useful energy.

solar system, hybrid *(système solaire hybride, m.)* A passive solar system that uses only a few mechanical devices to utilize the collected energy.

sole plate *(lisse d'assise, f.)* Bottom plate in timber framing.

solenoid valve *(vanne électromagnétique, f.)* A valve which is electrically operated.

Sound Transmission Class Acronym, STC *(indice de transmission du son ITS)* A system of ratings used to describe the performance of wall, floor and other assemblies in reducing airborne sound.

space heating See heating terms.

spalling *(écaillage, effritement, m.)* The breaking off of the surface layer of concrete or brick work, usually caused by frost action.

span *(portée, f.)* The horizontal distance between support beams, joists, rafters, etc. See also truss terminology.

special baths *(baignoire spéciale, f.)* Tubs with a built-in side opening door providing easier access for people who have difficulty in free movement. The door swings up or out and operates with a latch or button.

special purpose outlet See electrical terms.

special toilets *(toilette spéciale, f.)* Toilets that incorporate a regular cleansing spray or a soft mist spray, a warm water bidet and a hot air drier and automatic flusher.

specifications *(devis, m.)* Written document used with working drawings to provide information on the type and quality of materials and workmanship required for a project.

spillage *(fuite de gaz, f.)* The flow of combustion gases into the indoor air. This often follows or occurs simultaneously with backdrafting of vented appliances. Kerosene heaters, unvented heaters or fireplaces and most gas stoves and ovens spill into the indoor air.

splash block *(bloc parapluie, m.)* A small masonry block laid with the top close to the ground surface to receive roof drainage and divert it away from the building.

spline *(languette, f.)* A rectangular strip of wood which is substituted for the tongue fitted into the grooves of two adjoining members.

spores *(spores, f.)* Single cell capable of reproducing certain types of plant or plant-like life, including fungus.

spread *(portée, f.)* The horizontal width or diameter of the head of a tree or shrub.

springing line *(ligne de retombée, f.)* The point from which an arch, coved ceiling, or similar construction departs from vertical plane.

sprinkler *(arroser, m., asperseur, m.)* Device used to distribute water on grass, gardens or in buildings to stop a fire.

spunbonded olefin *(oléfine filée-liée, f.)* A fabric generally used to wrap the exterior of a house, often bonded to exterior glass fibre sheathing, to act as an air and wind barrier, preventing wind from reducing the effective RSI value of insulation.

sputtered See window terminology.

stack See plumbing terms.

stack effect *(effet de cheminée, m.)* A phenomenon caused by gravity where warm air rises in a house and exfiltrates through the upper half of the house, causing infliltration through the lower half of the house.

stack vent See plumbing terms.

staggered joints *(joints zigzagués ou en quinconce, m.)* Also known as broken joints. See joints.

staircase *(escalier, m.)* A flight of steps leading from one floor or storey to another above or below. The term includes landings, newel posts, handrails, and balustrades.

stair landing *(palier, m.)* A platform between flights of stairs.

stair lifts *(chaise-ascenseur, m.)* A chair or platform designed to glide up and down an extruded side riding rail or a monorail located near a staircase; used for people in wheelchairs or people with difficulty in moving.

stairway types *(escalier, m. (types))*

    enclosed *(escalier enfermé, m.)* A stairway enclosed by, and separated from, hallways and living units by means of walls or partitions and made accessible to such hallways or living units by means of a door or doors.

    interior *(escalier intérieur, m.)* A stairway within the exterior walls of a building.

    open *(escalier dégagé, m.)* A stairway which is not separated by walls and partitions from other areas in the building including hall ways.

steady state See heating terms.

steam heating See heating terms.

steel-frame construction See construction types.

steel stud *(poteau d'acier, m.)* Material mostly used to construct back up walls and partitions in high-rise buildings. It has the same dimensions as common wood studs except that it is made from bent and stamped thin steel sheet.

step flashing *(solin à gradins, m.)* Overlapping rectangular or square pieces of flashing used at the junction of a shingled roof and walls. Also called shingle flashing.

step joint Also known as broken joint. See joints.

steps *(marches, f.)* A wooden or concrete assembly that allows people to move from one elevation to another.

stile *(montant, m.)* A vertical piece of a sash, door, or piece of framing or panelling to which the ends of the rails are attached.

stonework, kinds of *(genres d'ouvrage de moellons, m.)* A type of construction where stones are used as masonry units.

ashlar *(pierre de taille, f.)* Masonry of sawn, dressed, tooled, or quarry-faced stone with proper bond.

broken ashlar *(pierre de taille irrégulière, f.)* Ashlar in which stones of different heights are used.

coursed ashlar *(pierre de taille par assises, f.)* Ashlar with stones laid to form courses around the building, all of the stones in any course being the same height.

coursed rubble *(moellons par assises, m.)* Construction using fieldstones placed in a continuous layer.

hammer-dressed ashlar *(pierre de taille bouchardée, f.)* Designates work where the stones are roughly squared with a hammer.

rubble *(moellon, m.)* Hand-picked or rough quarried stone of varying size and thickness.

rubblework *(ouvrage de moellons, m.)* Construction using broken fieldstone.

uncoursed rubble *(maçonnerie irrégulière, f.)* Construction where there is no attempt to align field stones in a continuous layer.

stool *(rebord de fenêtre, m.)* The flat, narrow shelf forming the top member of the interior trim at the bottom of a window.

stoop *(perron, m.)* A low platform with or without steps, outside the entrance door of a house.

storey. Also, story *(étage, m.)* The floor of a building or the habitable space between floors.

storey, first *(rez-de-chaussée, m.)* The storey with its floor closest to grade and having its ceiling more than 1800 mm above grade. In the United Kingdom, first storey refers to the floor above this.

storm See window types.

storm door *(contre-porte, f.)* An extra outside door for protection against inclement weather.

storm sewer See site drainage.

storm water See plumbing terms.

storm window See window types.

stove or muffler cement *(ciment pour poêle, m.)* A glue used in areas where high temperatures are present, and where there is no joint movement; usually used with other materials for air sealing around masonry or factory built chimneys.

stove, wood See wood stove.

strapping *(fond de clouage, m.)* A general term for battens fixed to the faces of walls as a support for lath and plaster or other cladding. See also furring.

street furniture *(mobilier urbain, m.)* Fittings and fixtures installed in streets, such as lamp posts, fire hydrants, street signs, and similar municipal structures at or above grade level.

stress *(contrainte, f.)* An internal force that resists a change in shape or size caused by external forces.

> **ultimate stress** *(contrainte ultime, f.)* The highest unit stress a piece of material can sustain at, or just before, rupture.

> **unit stress** *(contrainte unitaire pratique, f.)* The ultimate stress divided by a safety factor.

stress strap See electrical terms.

stretcher *(panneresse, f.)* A whole brick which has been laid so that its length is in line with the face of the wall.

stretching bond *(appareil de panneresses, m.)* The form of bond, in which every brick is laid as a stretcher, each vertical joint lying at the centres of the stretchers above and below.

stretching course *(assise en panneresses, f.)* An external or visible course of bricks which is made up entirely of stretchers.

strike plate *(gâche, f.)* The part of a door lock set which is fastened to the jamb.

stringer *(tirant, limon, m.)* (1) A long, heavy horizontal timber which connects upright posts in a structure and supports a floor. (2) The inclined member which supports the treads and risers of a stair.

strongback *(renfort, m.)* A wood batten fixed at right angles to the tops of cross framing members or ceiling joists in order to align and level them.

structural timber *(bois d'oeuvre de charpente, m.)* Timber used in construction to bear loads, and therefore graded on the basis of the suitability of the entire piece for that purpose.

strut *(étrésillon, m.)* (1) A structural member which is designed to resist longitudinal compressive stress such as members supporting a ridge beam or rafters. (2) A short column.

stucco *(stuc, m.)* Any cement-like material used as an exterior covering for walls and the like, put on wet and drying hard and durable. See also roughcast.

stud *(poteau, m.)* One of a series of wood structural members (usually 50 mm nominal thickness) used as supporting elements in walls and partitions. (Plural: studs or studding).

subdrain See plumbing terms.

subfloor *(sous-plancher, m.)* Boards or sheet material laid on joists to support the finished floor.

subflorescence *(subflorescence, f.)* A condition in masonry where mineral salts in crystalline form accumulate below the surface of masonry material. The accumulation and expansion of these salts create pressures which may result in the loss of surface material, exposing weaker material on the interior.

sub-grade *(sous-fondation, f.)* The prepared and compacted ground level which is to receive a pavement or topsoil; the end product of rough grading.

subsoil drainage pipe See plumbing terms.

subsurface drain See plumbing terms.

sump   See plumbing terms.

sump pump See plumbing terms.

superelevation *(surélévation, f.)* The elevation of the outside edge of a roadway curve, which is banked to reduce sideslipping of vehicles.

swale   See site drainage.

switch   See electrical terms.

T

T-rail   *(fer en té, m.)* A steel bar with a T-like cross section.

T-valve   See plumbing terms.

tactile strips *(bandes d'avertissement tactile, f.)* Raised lettering or textured surface strips to warn people with visual disabilities when a staircase begins and ends, or to warn of some other feature in the house design.

tail piece *(élément boîteux, m.)* A relatively short beam, joist, or rafter, supported on one end by a header.

tamp   *(damer, v.)* To compact soil or other material by applying repeated vertical blows, either manually or with a mechanical device.

tap   See faucet.

taping   *(pontage, m.)* In drywall construction, the finishing of joints between sheets by means of paper tape which is smoothed over with joint cement.

tar   *(goudron, m.)* A bituminous material, liquid or semi-solid, which has adhesive and waterproofing properties.

temperature control valve *(régulateur de température, m.)* A valve that ensures water temperature is never too hot or cold, especially useful for the kitchen sink, bath and shower, to predetermine the maximum or desired temperature.

temperature rods *(barres de dilatation, f.)* Small steel rods embedded in concrete to overcome cracking due to expansion and contraction.

tenon   *(tenon, m.)* The end of a piece of lumber formed to fit into a mortise.

tensile strength *(résistance à la traction, f.)* In structural work, the ability of a structure or structural members to resist tension.

tension   *(traction, f.)* The stress that resists the tendency of two forces acting away from each other, to pull apart two adjoining planes of a body.

terrace   *(terrasse, f.)* A raised level space having at least one upright or sloping side.

terrace home See house types.

terrazzo   *(terrazzo, m.)* A floor finish consisting of cement and marble granite chips, used over concrete, floated, ground, and polished to a smooth surface.

thermal break *(isolant thermique, m.)* Material of low conductivity used in a building assembly to reduce the flow of heat by conduction from one side of the assembly to the other. The term is often used to refer to materials used for this purpose in the frame of metal windows.

thermal bridge *(pont thermique, m.)* A low thermal resistance path connecting two surfaces - for example, framing members in insulated frame walls or metal ties in cavity wall and panel construction.

thermal envelope *(enveloppe thermique, f.)* A term referring to the insulated envelope of a living unit (walls, ceiling and/or floors) that protect it from the exterior temperature variations.

thermal insulation *(isolation thermique, f.)* A generic name for all insulation materials. See insulation.

thermal resistance value Also, R-Value *(Valeur de résistance thermique, f., valeur R)* A precise measurement of an insulation material's resistance to heat flow. The higher the resistance value, the slower the rate of heat transfer through the insulating material. Equivalent to the metric RSI.

thermal storage, phase change *(emmagasinage de chaleur latente, m.)* A heat-storage system based on materials such as eutectic salts, that change from solid to liquid as they absorb heat and revert from liquid to solid as they lose it.

thermal storage, rock bed *(emmagasinage de chaleur par une masse de gravier, m.)* An insulated container of small-size pebbles that retain solar heat for later use.

thermostat *(thermostat, m.)* An instrument, usually electrically operated, which responds to changes in temperature in a room or space and automatically controls the operation of a heating or cooling device.

thimble *(machon d'emboîtement, m., virole, f.)* A device to allow passage of a chimney section through a wall or ceiling.

three-way switch *(interrupteur tripolaire, m.)* See electrical terms.

threshold *(seuil, m.)* A strip of wood, metal, or other material, usually bevelled on each edge and used at the junction of two different floor finishes under doors, or on top of the door sill at exterior doors.

throat *(avaloir, f.)* The narrowing passage located between a fireplace and smoke chamber or flue.

tile *(tuile, f.)* (1) A surface covering made up of small pieces of ceramic or stone set in a grout or similar fixing material. (2) A small piece of ceramic or stone that is a component of a tiled surface. (3) A fired clay pipe or plate, often glazed to make it water resistant.

    ceramic *(carreau céramique, m.)* Decorative ceramic tiles of various shapes and sizes, normally used where excessive exposure to moisture could occur.

    flue *(boisseau, m.)* Glazed or unglazed tile about 600 mm either round, oblong, or square which lines the chimney flue.

    hearth *(carreau d'âtre, m.)* Unglazed machine-made tile about 12 mm thick to surface fireplace hearth.

    plumbing *(drain de semelle, m.)* Glazed tile, with bell joints for drains below grade.

    quarry *(carreau de carrière, m.)* Unglazed machine-made paving tile not less than 19 mm in thickness; also called promenade tile.

    roof *(tuile de toit, f.)* Unglazed machine-made tile in varying thickness and shapes to prevent the entry of water.

timber *(bois debout, m.)* (1) Standing trees of commercial size. (2) *(bois de sciage, m.)* Felled trees or logs suitable for sawing; as applied to manufactured wood. (3) *(bois d'oeuvre, m.)* A piece of lumber with a minimum dimension of 125 mm.

time delay fuse See electrical terms.

toenailing *(clouage en biais, m.)* Nailing at an angle to the first member so as to ensure penetration into a second member.

tongue-and-groove lumber *(bois embouveté, m.)* Any lumber, such as boards or planks, machined in such a manner that there is a groove on one edge and a corresponding tongue on the other.

tooled joint See joints.

topography *(topographie, f.)* The configuration of the surface of a site; its relief, landforms, and slopes.

top plate *(sablière, f.)* In building, the horizontal member nailed to the top of the partition or wall studs.

top soil See soil.

town house See house types.

track *(rail, m.)* An assembly used at the bottom and top of a steel stud wall to space the studs equally and hold them.

transfer seat *(chaise de transfert, f.)* A chair, sometimes based on a hydraulic system, which allows a person with a mobility disability to get into a bathtub by swinging the feet over the side and lowering themselves in. Can also refer to a similar system allowing a person with a mobility disability to get in and out of bed.

transformer See electrical terms.

transient See heating terms.

transmission loss See heating terms.

transom *(meneau d'imposte, m., imposte, f.)* (1) The horizontal bar which divides a window into heights or stages. (2) The opening above a door or window used for light or ventilation.

transplant *(transplanter, v.)* To move a plant from one location or container to another.

trap See plumbing terms.

trap seal See plumbing terms.

trap seal loss See plumbing terms.

tread *(marche, f.)* The horizontal part of a step, as opposed to the vertical riser.

trellis *(treillis, treillage, m.)* An open framework or lattice, used as a support for climbing plants.

trim *(boiserie, f.)* The finish materials in a building, such as moulding applied around openings, (window trim, door trim) or at the floor and ceiling of rooms (baseboard, cornice, picture moulding).

trimmer *(chevêtre, m.)* A beam or joist alongside an opening and into which a header is framed.

trombe wall *(mur trombe, m.)* A masonry or concrete wall behind large floor-to-ceiling glass or other glazing material; its purpose is to absorb and store solar heat to be used later.

trowelled surface *(surface truellée, f.)* A cement or mortar surface that has been given a smooth finish by means of a trowel.

truss *(ferme, f.)* A structural framework used in roofs and composed of a series of members so arranged and fastened together that external loads applied at the joints will cause only direct stress in the members.

truss terminology *(fermes, f. (terminologie))*

bay *(baie, f.)* The portion of the roof between two adjacent trusses.

bent *(portique, m.)* When a truss is supported at its ends by columns, the truss together with its columns, considered as a unit.

ceiling beams *(poutres de plafond, f.)* Beams supported by the lower chords, spanning between trusses and supporting the ceiling construction.

chord members *(membrures, f.)* The upper or lower flange members of a truss.

compression web members *(membrures d'âme comprimées, f.)* Those members which are subject to compression stress.

counter *(contre-fiche, f.)* A member of a truss system which acts only for a particular partial loading, and which has zero stress when the truss is completely loaded.

counter brace *(contre-tirant, m.)* A web member which is designed to resist either tension or compression.

panel or panel length *(longueur de panneau, f.)* The distance between two adjacent joints along either the upper or lower truss chords.

panel-point *(joint de ferme, m.)* The intersection of two or more members of the truss. Also called a joint.

pitch *(pente, f.)* The ratio of the vertical rise to the horizontal span. Also called slope. See also rise.

purlin *(panne, f.)* Beams supported by the upper chords, spanning from truss to truss, and supporting the roof construction.

rafter *(chevron, m.)* An inclined structural member of the roof, usually of 38 mm (1.5 inch) thickness, designed to support roof loads, but not ceiling finish.

rise *(montée, f.)* The distance between the apex or the highest point of the truss and the line joining the points of support.

slope *(pente, f.)* The ratio of the vertical rise to the horizontal run for inclines; generally expressed as 4 in 12, 6 in 12, etc.

span *(portée, f.)* The distance between the centres of the supports.

structural covering *(revêtement de charpente, m.)* The construction above the purlins, such as rafters and sheathing designed to support the weathering surface.

sub-purlin *(panne secondaire, f.)* A secondary system of beams parallel to the purlins and supported by the rafters; is sometimes employed to support tile or slate weathering surfaces.

web members *(membrures d'âme, f.)* Those members of a truss which are framed between, and join the upper and lower chords.

tuck-pointing *(rejointoiement, m.)* The finishing of mortar joints by cutting a groove in the surface of the joints and repointing or filling with mortar in a manner to provide a properly tooled joint.

twisted pair wire *(paire torsadée, f.)* A wire with two strands sheathed in plastic. Twisted pair allows two way communications and is typically found in older telephone systems.

Type D fuse See electrical terms, time delay fuse.

Type P fuse See electrical terms, low melting point fuse.

U

U factor *(valeur U, m.)* A measure of the propensity of a material or an assembly of materials to conduct heat, measured in watts per square metre per degree Celsius. The U factor is the inverse of the R-value, i.e., $U = 1/R$.

ULV Acronym for Ultra Low Volume *(à bas volume)* Term used to describe water-conserving amenities as in a ULV toilet or ULV showerhead.

ultimate stress See stress.

unit stress See stress.

unvented space See heating terms.

urea formaldehyde *(urée-formaldéhyde, f.)* A synthetic compound made by condensing urea with formaldehyde and used in adhesives, moulded articles and finishes.

urea formaldehyde foam insulation (UFFI) *(mousse isolante d'urée-formaldéhyde, f. MIUF)* A form of foam insulation blown into existing walls.

urethane foam sealant *(matériau d'étanchéité à l'uréthane, m.)* An insulating foam ideal for filling larger joints and cavities where conventional sealant materials may not be suitable such as around plumbing and vent openings. Ventilation is required during installation.

utilities *(infrastructure, f., équipements d'infrastructure, m.)* Public and private services such as water, telephone, electricity, and sewage disposal. Also called infrastructure.

V

VOC Acronym for Volatile Organic Compound. *(COV composé organique volatif, m.)* One of a group of organic chemicals that can be a gas or vapour at indoor temperature and are found in a variety of common products such as oil-based paints and varnishes, caulking, glues, synthetic carpeting and vinyl flooring, etc. They contribute to poor indoor air quality.

vacuum breaker See plumbing terms.

valance *(boîte à rideaux, f.)* A decorative board across a window head, fastened to the wall, used to conceal the top of window curtains.

valley *(noue, f.)* The internal angle formed by the junction of two sloping surfaces of a roof.

valley rafters See rafter types.

valve *(soupape, f.)* A device by which the flow of liquid or gas can be regulated by a moveable part which either closes, opens or obstructs the passage.

vanity *(meuble-lavabo, f.)* A counter or cabinet to support a basin or sink in a bathroom or lavatory.

vapour barrier *(pare-vapeur, m.)* Material used in the house envelope to retard the passage of water vapour or moisture. The performance is rated in perms.

vapour diffusion *(diffusion de vapeur, f.)* The movement of water vapour between two areas caused by a difference in vapour pressure, independent of air movement. The rate of diffusion is determined by (1) the difference in vapour pressure; and (2) the permeability of the material to water vapour (hence the selection of materials of low permeability for use as vapour diffusion retarders in buildings).

vapour retarder *(pare-vapeur, m.)* Material (or system) used in the house envelope to retard the passage of water vapour or moisture through materials. The performance is rated in perms. Also referred to as vapour barrier and vapour diffusion retarder.

varnish See paint.

vehicle See paint.

veneer *(placage, m.)* A thin piece or layer of wood of uniform thickness applied to a back-up material.

veneer (masonry) See masonry types.

vent *(reniflard, m.)* An opening for passage or escape or relieving pressure of fluid, gas or smoke.

vent (gas) *(évent, m.)* A pipe connected to a gas appliance to conduct the products of combustion to the outside air.

vented appliance *(appareil ventilé, m.)* An indirect-fired appliance provided with a flue collar to accommodate a chimney connector for conveying flue gases to the outside air.

vent damper device, automatic *(registre de tirage clapet, m.)* A device intended for installation in the venting system, in the outlet of, or downstream of the appliance draft hood, of an individual, automatically operated, gas-fired appliance and which is designed to automatically open the venting system when the appliance is in operation, and to automatically close off the venting system when the appliance is in a standby or shutdown condition.

vent stack See plumbing terms.

vented space heater See heating terms.

ventilation *(ventilation, f.)* The movement of outdoor air through a building's exterior envelope via leaks or intended openings, both inward and outward (infiltration and exfiltration). Ventilation is measured in air changes per hour. See air change.

    circulation *(circulation, f.)* The movement of air within rooms or confined spaces.

    distribution *(distribution, f.)* The transfer of ventilation air into and out of rooms or other confined spaces inside a building's envelope.

ventilation loss *(déperdition de chaleur par ventilation, f.)* Heat loss by exfiltration through holes in a structure.

venting system See plumbing terms.

verge board *(bordure de pignon, f.)* The board under the edge of gables, sometimes moulded. Also called barge board. See also facer board.

vermiculite *(vermiculite, m.)* A mineral closely related to mica, having the property, when heated, of expanding to give it insulating properties. It is used as bulk insulation and also as an aggregate in plaster.

vertical curve *(courbe verticale, f.)* A road curve in the vertical plane.

vestibule See house rooms.

veranda See outdoor spaces.

vibrating alarm *(avertisseur vibrant, m.)* Portable warning device that vibrates when a doorbell rings or some other household function is performed; useful for people with limitations to hearing or vision, people with mobility impairments and people who are bed-ridden.

visible alarm *(avertisseur visuel, m.)* Warning device equipped with a flashing light; useful to people who are hard-of-hearing or deaf; also desirable where quiet is important.

voltage See electrical terms.

W

waferboard *(panneau de grandes particules, m.)* Structural wood panel manufactured from wood wafers or strands bonded together with glue. It is a high strength product made from low grade (waste) material. Also called chipboard.

wall, common *(mur commun, m.)* A vertical separation completely dividing a portion of a structure from the remainder of the structure.

wall plate *(lisse, f.)* In wood-frame construction, the horizontal members attached to the ends of the studs. Also called top or bottom plates, depending on their location.

wane *(flache, f.)* Bark or lack of wood on the edge or corner of a piece of lumber.

warp *(gauchissement, m.)* Any variation from a true surface such as bow, cup, twist, etc., generally resulting from defective seasoning.

waste audit *(vérification des déchets, f.)* A comprehensive analysis of the waste produced by any given workplace or institution. Audits often reveal areas where waste can be reduced or recycled.

waste management *(gestion des déchets, f.)* The establishment and control of the unused byproducts of a process or garbage produced during a process; often includes planning to reduce waste, re-use waste and recycling.

water bar *(cassis, m.)* A bar set in the joint between the wood sill and masonry, or wood sill and sash of a window, to prevent penetration of water. Also called weather bar.

water closet See plumbing terms.

water filter *(filtre à eau, m.)* A device or system externally connected to a water source that removes particulates to help purify water.

water hammer See plumbing terms.

water meter *(compteur d'eau, m.)* A device for measuring the quantity of water passing through a water service.

water preheat tank *(réservoir d'eau réchauffée au préalable, m.)* A vessel used to store water which is heated by alternative means such as passive solar heat before it is fed into the domestic hot water tank.

waterproof membrane *(membrane imperméable, f.)* Sheet materials applied to a roof or wall surface to prevent the penetration of water, often in several layers or "plies".

water retrofit *(modernisation de la plomberie, f.)* The replacement of existing water fixtures and appliances with water-conserving fixtures and appliances. Water retrofits can involve a wide range of approaches including low-flow six litre toilets, low-flow shower heads and faucet aerators, and rain barrel collectors for gardens.

water service pipe See plumbing terms.

water table *(nappe aquifère, f.)* **(1)** The level below which the ground is saturated with water. **(2)** *(rejeteau, m.)* A ledge or offset on or above a foundation wall formed to shed water.

water vapour *(vapeur d'eau, f.)* Water in a gaseous state, present in the atmosphere in varying amounts.

water vapour permeance *(perméance à la vapeur d'eau, f.)* The rate at which water vapour diffuses through a sheet of any thickness of material (or assembly between parallel surfaces). It is the ratio of water vapour flow to the differences of the vapour pressures on the opposite surfaces. Permeance is measured in perms (ng/Pa_s_m² or grain/ft²hr (in_Hg).

water vapour pressure *(pression de vapeur d'eau, f.)* The pressure exerted by water vapour in the air and proportional to the absolute amount of water in the air. Water vapour moves from an area of high pressure to an area of low pressure.

watt See electrical terms.

weather bar See water bar.

weather check *(coupe-larme, m.)* A groove on the under side of a projecting member to form a drip to prevent rain from running down the wall or entering the joint.

weatherization *(imperméabilisation, f.)* A minor retrofit involving the installation of relatively low cost items such as weather-stripping of doors and windows and air-sealing designed to improve the tightness of a building against energy loss due to wind and cold.

weatherstripping *(coupe-bise, m.)* Strips of felt, rubber, metal, or other material, fixed along the edges of doors or windows to keep out drafts and reduce heat loss.

web connection *(construction à réseau triangulé, f.)* In construction, a method of assembling steel stud walls where the studs are secured to the top track with a flexible clip to free the backup wall from vertical loads, but still support horizontal loads. See backup, and track.

web member See truss terminology.

weephole *(trou d'évacuation d'eau, m.)* A small hole, as at the bottom of a retaining wall or masonry veneer, to drain water to the exposed face.

weeping tile *(tuyaux de drainage, f.)* Perforated pipes connected to a foundation drain below the surface of the ground to collect water from the foundation of a building.

weir See plumbing terms.

wet vent See plumbing terms.

wind barrier *(pare-vent, m.)* A textile or fabric wrap located on the outside of a building envelope to protect insulation from the circulation of outside air. See spunbonded olefin.

wind effect *(pression du vent, f.)* A condition which exists when wind blows against a house, creating a high pressure area on the windward side forcing air into the house. Simultaneously, a low pressure area is present on the leeward and sometimes other sides of the house.

winder *(marche d'angle, f.)* A step, generally triangular in plan, used at a change in direction of a stair.

window, parts of *(fenêtres, m. (constituants))*

> **balance** *(contrepoids, m.)* A device used to counteract the weight of the sash for ease of operation.

> **light** *(carreau, m.)* Window pane; the term is used to designate the number of separate panes which make up the entire window.

> **lintel** *(linteau, m.)* The horizontal top piece of the window framework.

> **mullion** *(meneau, m.)* The perpendicular members which divide the bays or lights of windows or screen-work.

> **muntin** *(meneau, montant, m.)* A horizontal member which divides lights of glass, windows, or doors.

> **pane** *(vitrage, m.)* A glass surface in a window. A window may include a number of panes or may consist of a single pane.

> **rough frame** *(cadre brut, m.)* Framing of the enclosure in which the finished window frame is placed.

> **sash** *(châssis, m.)* A light frame of wood, metal, or plastic either fixed or movable which holds the glass. See sash types.

> **sill** *(seuil de fenêtre, m.)* The base of the window frame sloped on the outside to shed rain.

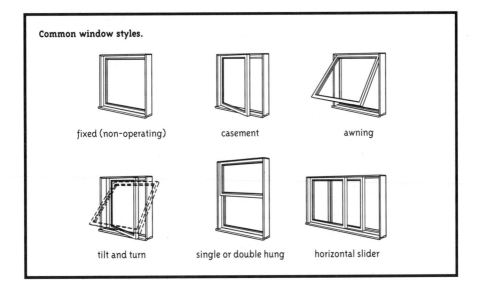

Common window styles.

fixed (non-operating)   casement   awning

tilt and turn   single or double hung   horizontal slider

window terminology *(fenêtres, m. (terminologie))*

> **awning window** *(fenêtre-auvent, f.)* A frame containing one or more sash, each of which is installed in a vertical plane and is hinged to permit the bottom of the sash to open outward.
>
> **bay window** *(fenêtre en baie, f.)* Window which projects outside the main line of a building and the compartment in which it is located.
>
> **bow window** *(fenêtre en baie ronde, f.)* A type of bay window that is curved rather than angled.
>
> **casement window** *(fenêtre à battants, f.)* A frame which contains a sash hinged at the side to open in or out.
>
> **check rail window** *(fenêtre à traverse mobile, f.)* A frame containing at least a pair of sashes which are engaged when closed. The sashes are installed in a vertical plane and designed to be moved either vertically or horizontally.
>
> **checker window** *(fenêtre à carreaux, f.)* An old style window consisting of small muntins and mullions holding small panes of glass; several of these panes are present in one window.
>
> **clerestory window** *(fenêtre haute, f.)* A window which occurs in the wall of a clerestory.
>
> **dormer window** *(lucarne, f.)* A vertical window in a dormer for lighting a room adjoining a sloping roof.
>
> **double glazed** *(double vitrage, m.)* Window made of two layers of glass separated by an air space to increase its thermal resistance (RSI).
>
> **double-hung window** *(fenêtre à l'anglaise, f.)* A window with an upper and lower sash, each balanced by springs or weights to be capable of vertical movement with relatively little effort.
>
> **ER** *(CEE)* An energy rating system developed for windows and sliding doors which compares the amount of energy lost through air leakage and through the glass, spacers and frames with the amount of heat gained through solar gain . It is expressed in watts per square metre and can be a negative or positive number. A typical ER number of a single glazed window is -50, for double glazed -30, and for low-e argon filled between -12 and +4.
>
> **fire window** *(fenêtre coupe-feu, f.)* A window with its frame, sash, and glazing which, under standard test conditions, meets the fire protection requirements for the location in which it is to be used.
>
> **gas-filled windows** *(fenêtre remplie de gaz, f.)* Sealed window unit (double or triple-glazed) in which a heavier-than-air and inert gas, usually argon, but can be krypton, is used to replace the air between the glazings. This results in an improved thermal performance of the window.
>
> **hopper window** *(fenêtre-tremie, f.)* A frame containing one or more sash, each of which is installed in a vertical plane and hinged to permit the top of the sash to open inwards.
>
> **jalousie window** *(fenêtre-jalousie, f.)* A frame containing a number of movable, shutter-like, overlapping glass panels.

window terminology (continued)

low-emissivity (Low-E) *(fenêtre à faible émissivité, f.)* A window with a thin metal coating applied to the glazing to reduce the amount of heat radiated. Low-e windows are designed to help keep the inside cool in summer and warm in winter. See also pyrolytic and sputtered.

oriel window *(fenêtre en encorbellement, f.)* A window or group of windows that projects beyond the wall of a building and is usually carried on brackets or corbels.

Palladian window *(fenêtre serlienne, f.)* A window featuring a semi-circular pane over a rectangular pane; named for 16th Century Italian architect Andrea Palladio.

pyrolytic *(fenêtre pyrolitique, f.)* Hard low-e coatings on the glass in a window, applied by fusing tin oxide to the surface of molten glass; they are very durable.

sashless window *(fenêtre sans châssis, f.)* A window with a wood frame containing at least two lights of glass with polished or ground edges, or sash with light metal or plastic edges. At least one light of glass slides horizontally or vertically.

sputtered *(fenêtre à pulvérisation cathodique, f.)* Soft low-e coatings on the glass in a window produced by coating a glazing surface with silver or zinc atoms in a vacuum; they are easily damaged, and must be protected during the manufacturing process.

storm window *(contre-châssis, m.)* A full-length window with either fixed or movable sashes, fitted to the outside of a window frame to afford protection during cold or stormy weather.

transom window *(imposte, f., vasistas, m.)* A horizontal rectangular window set above a door or another window.

triple glazed *(triple vitrage, m.)* Window made of three layers of glass separated by air spaces to increase its thermal resistance (RSI).

U-value *(coefficient K, m.)* The overall amount of heat transmitted through the entire window (centre of glass, edge of glass, frame, and spacer).

visible transmittance *(transmittance, f.)* The amount of light that a window lets through. Visible transmittance is often compromised by energy efficient features such as multiple glazings, low-e.

wire nails See nails, types of.

wire connector See connector, wire.

wired glass *(verre armé, m.)* Glass reinforced by a layer of wire mesh.

wiring See electrical terms.

wood-frame construction See construction types.

wood framing *(charpenterie, f.)*

balloon framing *(ossature à claire-voie, f.)* A method of wood-frame construction in which the studs extend in one piece from the foundation wall to the top plate supporting the roof.

braced framing *(charpente contreventée, f.)* The extensive use of planks and nails rather than more expensive heavy timbers, mortise and tenon joints. Also known as half frame.

Wall framing used with platform construction: *(1)* top plate end-nailed to each stud with two 3 1/4 in. (82 mm) nails; *(2)* top plates nailed together with 3 in. (76 mm) nails 24 in. (600 mm) on centre; *(3)* stud toenailed with four 2 1/2 in. (63 mm) nails or end-nailed to bottom plate with two 3 1/4 in. (82 mm) nails; *(4)* top plates at corners and loadbearing partitions are lapped and nailed together with two 3 1/4 in. (82 mm) nails or the plates are butted together and tied with a metal plate fastened to the top plates with three 2 1/2 in. (63 mm) nails on each side of the joint; *(5)* doubled studs at openings and multiple studs at corners and intersections nailed with 3 in. (76 mm) nails 30 in. (750 mm) on centre; *(6)* bottom plate nailed to joist or header joist with 3 1/4 in. (82 mm) nails 16 in. (400 mm) on centre.

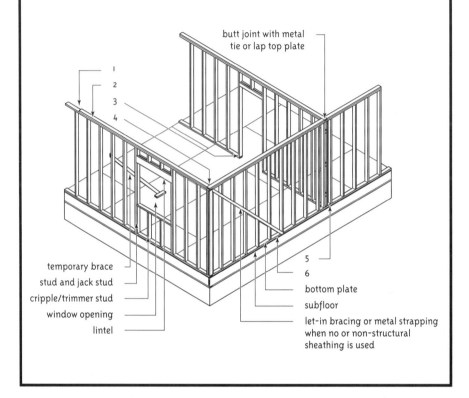

butt joint with metal tie or lap top plate

1
2
3
4

temporary brace
stud and jack stud
cripple/trimmer stud
window opening
lintel

5
6
bottom plate
subfloor
let-in bracing or metal strapping when no or non-structural sheathing is used

wood framing (continued)

bridging *(entretoise, f.)* A method used to resist twisting of joists and for stiffening floor construction by fitting either crossed pieces or solid blocks between the joists.

cap *(couronnement, m.)* The upper half of the top plate in wood-frame walls and partitions.

full framing *(ossature en bois d'oeuvre, f.)* A framework of squared timbers held together with systems of pinned mortise and tenon joints. Also called timber framing.

half frame See braced framing.

wood framing (continued)

plank framing *(charpente en madriers, f.)* A type of construction which employs flat vertical structural members with horizontal beams let into them and having an infilling of planks on edge.

platform framing See western framing.

post and beam framing *(charpente à poteaux et à poutres, f.)* A system of construction in which posts and beams support the loads and the infilling walls are non-load bearing.

timber framing See full framing.

western framing (platform framing) *(charpente de l'Ouest, f.)* A system of framing a building on which floor joists of each storey rest on the top of plates of the storey below (or on the foundation sill for the first storey) and the bearing walls and partitions rest on the subfloor of each storey.

wood lath *(latte de bois, f.)* Thin narrow piece of wood used as a base for plaster or stucco.

wood preservative *(préservatif pour le bois, m.)* A chemical product used to prevent or halt decay in exterior wood work. Applied by pressure treatment, soaking, or brush.

wood sleepers *(sous-poutre, f.)* Wood blocks used in insulated basement slab assemblies, replacing the insulation on the floor in strategic locations to support the walls of the basement.

wood stove *(poêle à bois, m.)* A wood-burning space heating device.

wythe *(paroi de mur à cavité, f.)* A continuous vertical section of a masonry wall having a thickness of one masonry unit.

X

X-10 A home automation protocol that uses existing AC wiring for communication between control devices and receiver modules. One of the oldest and most common home automation protocols, X-10 systems allow only one-way communication and very little processing power.

Y

yard *(jardin, m.)* The property or lot upon which a house is placed.

yard lumber *(bois de cour, m.)* Air dried lumber used for ordinary building purposes.

year ring *(anneau de croissance annuelle, m.)* One of the clearly defined rings in a cross section of a tree trunk showing the amount of annual growth of the tree. Each ring represents one year growth. See also annual growth ring.

Young's modulus See modulus of elasticity.

Z

zone heating *(chauffage de zones, m.)* A system of air and hydronic temperature management which relies on setting up sections of the interior of a building as zones, controlling each zone individually through multiple thermostats, valves and control devices on heating vents.

zone thermostat *(thermostat de zone, m.)* Thermostat that uses sensors located inside and outside of the house to sense the need for heat and cooling, and adjust the temperature accordingly; useful in reducing energy consumption.

zone ventilation *(ventilation de zone, f.)* A system of air distribution management which relies on setting up sections of the interior of a building as zones, controlling each zone individually through multiple sensors.